It Takes All Sorts

The sequel to
Voltaire, Goldberg and Others

A compendium of the eccentric, the hilarious and the wise

Milton Shulman

HOUSE OF STRATUS

Illustrations by Vicky

This edition published in 2003 by House of Stratus, an imprint of House of Stratus Ltd, Thirsk Industrial Park, York Road, Thirsk, North Yorkshire, YO7 3BX, UK.

www.houseofstratus.com

Typeset by House of Stratus.
Printed and bound in Great Britain by
Antony Rowe Ltd, Chippenham, Wiltshire

A catalogue record for this book is available from the British Library and the Library of Congress.

ISBN 0-7551-1142-7

Milton Shulman was born in Toronto, the son of a shopkeeper, and qualified as a lawyer. He spent five years in the Canadian Army, leaving with the rank of Major and was mentioned in Dispatches for his work as an intelligence officer in the invasion of France. Based upon his interrogation of senior German officers such as Field Marshal von Rundstedt and Colonel General Student, he wrote the classic work *Defeat in the West*, which was published in 1947 and is still in print.

He arrived for his first day at the *Evening Standard* in 1947, due largely to a series of fortuitous accidents. For the next 50 years he wrote about theatre, film, TV and politics, with a sharp humour and irreverence, for the *Evening Standard, Express, Spectator* and *Vogue*. For 18 years his distinctive Canadian tones were a regular feature of BBC Radio 4's witty and pungent talk show *Stop the Week*. A champion of quality and scourge of poor writing, he began by observing the British with an Atlantic detachment and amused bafflement, but has now become as important a landmark of London as the shiny black cab.

In order to understand the language and activities of the British he became a dedicated reader of British magazines and newspapers. His collection of the writings and observations of authors and journalists appeared recently in a compendium called *Voltaire, Goldberg and Others*. The demand for it was so great that it was reprinted three times within a period of a single year. *It Takes All Sorts* is an inevitable sequel to that quotation book and contains the same quality of reflections, observations and witticisms as in the previous volume.

His film and theatre reviews were a subject of much controversy. He has also written two books on TV, three novels and three children's books. He lives in London with his wife, the Modern Manners expert Drusilla Beyfus. His daughter Alexandra is the editor of British *Vogue*, his daughter Nicola has just written a much-praised book called *A Rage for Rock Gardening* and his son Jason is an art director and designer.

BY THE SAME AUTHOR

General

Defeat in the West
How to be a Celebrity
The Least Worst Television in the World
Marilyn, Hitler and Me
The Ravenous Eye
Voltaire, Goldberg and Others

Novels

Every Home Should Have One (with Herbert Kretzmer)
Kill Three
The Victors (Story of a Carl Foreman Film)

Children's Books

Preep
Preep and the Queen
Preep in Paris

To my noble brother
Alex

★ ☆ ★

Contents

List Of Illustrations By Vicky

Introduction

The gratifying reception of my first book of quotations, *Voltaire, Goldberg and Others* – it achieved a third printing in less than nine months – has prompted this sequel. Again the emphasis is on the writing of journalists, with obeisance to classical humorists like Groucho Marx, Dorothy Parker, Oscar Wilde and Noël Coward whose wit will continue to delight generations still to come. Although my first book spanned fifty years of reading of newspapers, journals and books, this volume has the majority of entries culled from the decade of the 1990s. Again it includes the work of such conjurors of the written word as Paul Johnson, John Walsh, Bernard Levin, Philip Norman, Craig Brown, Keith Waterhouse, A A Gill, Howard Jacobson, Zoe Heller, Victor Lewis-Smith, Jeffrey Bernard and Taki, which stands up to the great essayists and journalists of the past such as G K Chesterton, Hilaire Belloc, Harold Nicholson, Stephen Leacock, Swift, Hazlitt and Beerbohm.

One of the most chilling and moving contributions is George Orwell's account of his stay in a Paris hospital in 1929 from his essay 'How the Poor Die'. Paul Johnson's piece on gardens is a masterly reflection on an activity enjoyed by millions. The emphasis in this volume may be on slightly longer extracts than before (300 to 400 words) to give the writing the necessary space to make its impact. But the bulk of items will still, I believe, have that same sense of the absurd, the eccentric and the hilarious as *Voltaire, Goldberg and Others*. Again, to my surprise, I have discovered another cache of Jewish jokes which stand up to the bizarre and funny selection in the earlier volume of this specialised brand of ethnic humour.

Although I was chastised by one critic for daring to have my name credited with so many quotations in the Index (most of them were only there to credit somebody else's wit as the source), I have taken the liberty in this volume to include two items from my memoirs, *Marilyn, Hitler and Me*, which have attracted much amused comment from readers of that volume. The first describes my meeting with Lord Beaverbrook which started me on my critical career. The other I believe is a revealing bit of contemporary lore about the world of hype and commercial exploitation to which the tragic figure of Marilyn Monroe was subjected during her brief but tempestuous life.

My main object in having any of these quotations and extracts re-published in these two volumes is to save them from the shredding machine or some remote mausoleum for dead newspapers. In this regard I trust I have been reasonably successful as a literary embalmer. For those needing an explanation or a warning about this book before purchasing it, I can only reiterate the concluding words of my Introduction to *Voltaire, Goldberg and Others*. 'In the last analysis I must take the responsibility or the blame for what I have selected for my compendium. Readers who share my sense of humour, love the incongruous, are amused by the eccentric, are in awe of the profound, dazzled by the quick-witted, diverted by the accidental, enchanted by gracious writing, should, I hope, find a great deal of entertainment in these pages.'

1 They Aren't What They Seem

actors and acting

A new biography of the Cockney actor, Michael Caine, reveals him to be something of a prude, especially when it comes to taking his clothes off. 'I think that nudity is undignified,' he reveals in the book written by Michael Freedland. 'I think nude men look ridiculous, I really do. I didn't spend twenty years learning how to do something in order to have people staring at my bottom.' And what inspired this outburst? The revelation that he was offered the chance to play alongside Glenda Jackson in Ken Russell's film *Women in Love*.

• Mark Inglefield, Diary, *The Times* 29.12.99

★ ☆ ★

Hedy Lamarr, who has died aged 86, appeared stark naked in the widely banned film *Ecstasy* of 1933, and was Delilah to Victor Mature's Samson in Cecil B De Mille's biblical epic of 1949.

These were the twin peaks of a career that otherwise attracted little critical attention. For many years she was under contract to MGM, whose studio boss, Louis B Mayer, thought she would be bigger than Garbo. But her dark, sensuous looks always figured more prominently in press notices than her acting ability. 'She didn't have an ego problem,' noted the director John Cromwell. 'The problem was she couldn't act.'

Like many Hollywood stars, she was married several times, notching up six husbands and many more lovers. The most interesting of her romantic associations was with the *avant garde* composer George Antheil, who had written the incidental score to the 1924 silent film *Ballet Mécanique* and whom she first met at a party in 1940.

There was immediate chemistry when she asked him how she could enlarge her breasts, but he soon realized he was dealing with a superior intellect, for the conversation progressed rapidly to military technology. It was a meeting of minds, and between them Antheil and Hedy Lamarr went on to patent a communications device.

Apparently they were strumming at the piano one evening when she noticed that they were 'talking' to one another and could follow each other's lead despite constantly shifting key, though to untuned ears it would have sounded a jumble. In her imagination Hedy Lamarr made the leap that would enable the principle to be applied equally to military use. At any rate, they were granted a patent in 1942 for a 'secret communication system'.

The US Navy of the day, however, was unimpressed, especially when it transpired that the system would involve submarines carrying piano rolls to baffle the enemy's decoders. So Hedy's brainwave languished until the patent expired in 1959. Three years later, however, 'frequency-hopping' was used in the Cuban crisis and later became the basis of America's Milstar defence system. That, at least, was how the actress recalled it, basking in an intellectual Indian summer after Hans-Joachim Braun, of Hamburg University, had stumbled upon the original patent.

• *Daily Telegraph* 20.1.00

★ ☆ ★

There's a very good joke about Marilyn Monroe when she married Arthur Miller. They were engaged then. He said, 'I would like you to meet my mother, she would like to see you. So I thought we'd go to her little apartment in the Bronx, we'll have a little dinner, and she'll get to know you.' And Marilyn said, 'Wonderful, wonderful.'

So they go there, to that tiny little apartment, with a kind of very flimsy door between the living room and the toilet. They're having a very good time, they get along great, and then Marilyn Monroe says she's got to go to the WC, the toilet. And she goes, and because the walls are thin, she turns on all the faucets so they would not hear it in the next room.

Now she comes out, and everything's beautiful, kiss, kiss, kiss. Next day, Arthur calls the mother and says, 'How did you like her?' And the mother says, 'She's sweet, a wonderful, wonderful, wonderful girl, but she pisses like a horse!'

• *Conversations with Billy Wilder* by Cameron Crowe.
Extracts from *Daily Telegraph* 8.11.99

★ ☆ ★

She had a kind of elegant vulgarity about her. That, I think, was very important, and she automatically knew where the joke was. She did not discuss it. She came for the first rehearsal, and she was absolutely perfect, when she remembered the line. She could do a three-page dialogue scene perfectly, and then get stuck on a line like: 'It's me, Sugar.' We spent quite a few takes getting: 'It's me, Sugar!' I had signs painted on the door: IT'S ME, SUGAR. 'Action' would come and she would say, 'It's Sugar, me!' I took her to the side after about take 50; and I said, 'Don't worry about it.' And she said, 'Worry about what?' (*Shakes head.*) The 50th take, that was, and then there was the 51st, and the 52nd…

• *Ibid*

★ ☆ ★

It Takes All Sorts

Marilyn Monroe committed suicide yesterday. The usual overdose. Poor silly creature. I am convinced that what brought her to that final foolish gesture was a steady diet of intellectual pretentiousness pumped into her over the years by Arthur Miller and 'The Method'. She was, to begin with, a fairly normal little sexpot with exploitable curves and a certain natural talent. I am sure all the idiocies of her last few years, always being late on set etc., plus over-publicity and too many theoretical discussions about acting, were the result of all this constant analysis of every line in every part she ever had to play and a desperate longing to be 'intellectual' without the brain to achieve it. It is a sad comment on contemporary values that a beautiful, famous and wealthy young women of 36 should capriciously kill herself for want of a little self-discipline and horse-sense.

• Noël Coward, 6 August 1962, quoted from the *Faber Book of Diaries* in the *Independent on Sunday*, 11.1998

★ ☆ ★

Antony (in Shakespeare's *Antony and Cleopatra*) is an absolute twerp. He doesn't have a lot between the ears. He grubs around the Nile and makes a cock-up of everything. If you play him, just remember, she's got you firmly by the balls.

• Laurence Olivier, quoted by Robert Butler, *Independent on Sunday*, 11.10.98

★ ☆ ★

'We used to have actresses trying to become stars,' Olivier once loftily remarked. 'Now we have stars trying to become actresses.'

• *Sunday Times*, 13.9.98

★ ☆ ★

On tour, actors gather round one table endlessly boozing, boring themselves into a numb zone. Most know when to stop, but there is always the one for whom booze acts as an incendiary device blowing part of his brain up. He fixes you with his newly acquired freedom, runny eyes pinning you in an accusing stare for being so stiff, reserved or sober. You feel guilty for not sharing this abandoned joy, his uninhibited release. Curiously, we other actors are involuntarily forced into a kind of submission, admiring his outrageous antics. His idiotic boldness we see as courage. We feel lesser as he grows bigger.

I was sucked into it as a young actor when the pub did nothing but sell booze, and maybe a few crisps to soak up the river of beer. We would dash desperately to the pub after the show, terrified lest we should miss our alcoholic reward. Like those newborn turtles racing for the sea, we raced to the pub.

We can get wrecked, since the acting profession is about the only job, apart from pop and rock perhaps, where you can perform the work pissed out of your mind. With memorising and repetition, once the words have sunk into your brain no amount of alcohol can budge them. They become like a tattoo that you can't remove.

Booze is taken for granted, almost like the rum station for sailors. I have to have a drink after a show as if to replace something, or even keep that sense of freedom going; however, I can't feel comfortable with the idea that the liver, kidney and brain are invincible.

• Steven Berkoff, *Independent*, 21.1.99

★ ☆ ★

The death-knell for political correctness sounds ever louder in America. For Annette Bening, liberal actress and wife of Warren Beatty, has struck out against PC in a letter to *Campus: America's Student Newspaper*.

According to US reporters, the cause is the absurd behaviour of her alma mater, Arizona State University.

It Takes All Sorts

The ASU Theatre Department, according to reporters, recently fired the head of its graduate acting programme, Professor Jared Skaren. Skaren's former pupils include Val Kilmer and Frances McDormand, as well as Annette Bening.

Skaren's crime, it seems, was teaching Shakespeare and Ibsen. His department head accused him of using 'works from a sexist European canon that is approached traditionally'.

The crunch for Skaren came when he was told to abandon Shakespeare in favour of a play called *Betty the Yeti: An Eco-Fable* in which a logger forms an inappropriate relationship with a sasquatch and is turned into an environmentalist.

• Peterborough, *Daily Telegraph* 5.10.98

★ ☆ ★

Think of 'I don't consider any girl perfect until she rejects me.' Or 'Don't knock masturbation – it's sex with someone I love.' They and a hundred other effortless but telling quips carry the unmistakeable stamp of Woody Allen, a copyright blend of existential whining, tortured self-love and some of the greatest comic writing ever created.

• J G Ballard reviewing *Woody Allen: A Biography* by John Baxter, *Daily Telegraph*, 14.11.98

★ ☆ ★

Do we all have a horror of comedians? I remember once shrivelling at the chance of meeting Peter Sellers for fear of being unable to laugh. The story of the Marx Brothers convinces you that you have to be psychotic to pursue merriment as a profession. Yet engaging glimpses of these jokers shine through all the showbiz tinsel draped over every page. They took revenge on Chaplin for reading a newspaper during a performance of theirs by hiring four Hassidic Jews to sit through one of his; the fundamentalists walked out, leaving Chaplin convinced they were the Marx Brothers in disguise. On meeting H G Wells, Harpo informed him that branches of Wells-Fargo existed all over the United States. Tongue in cheek?

How surreal were their high jinks? With grandiose lack of humour Salvador Dali wrote a screenplay for them called *Giraffes on Horseback Salad*. It was never made. Artaud twisted his brains into a knot to offer them a compliment so intellectual as to smack of insult. But really they were just anarchy running riot. They were chaos witticised. And as performers, or even as men, they were soon beyond all human control. 'Nobody could be at ease with the Marx Brothers,' said their cameraman, and even their director had to be 'quiet as a mouse pissing on a blotter'. However comic they were on stage or film, their private lives were laughable.

• David Hughes, reviewing *Monkey Business: the Lives and Legends of the Marx Brothers* by Simon Louvish, *Spectator*, 4.12.99

★ ☆ ★

Like Chaplin and Groucho Marx before him, Woody Allen has created a character cinema audiences find it impossible to forget; the funny, sensitive, endearing neurotic little man who is overwhelmed by mechanical gadgets – and women – but who nonetheless manages to survive and enjoy himself. He has become the personification of urban anxiety.

This slight 5 ft 5 in. Jewish New Yorker, now 49, with thinning red hair and brown eyes that peer out sceptically from behind thick glasses, has become one of the cinema's least likely heroes: the antithesis of the matinee idol movie star.

A short story writer as well as a performer, Allen has also coined some of the wittiest sayings of recent times. On death, 'It's not that I'm afraid to die. I just don't want to be there when it happens.' On suicide, 'There have been times when I've thought about it – but with my luck it would probably turn out to be only a temporary solution.' And on sex, 'The most fun I ever had without laughing.'

* ☆ *

Nothing, not even race or language, divides the world into factions more than comedy. What penetrates the human spirit with more enlightenment and wisdom then humour? I always found Chaplin arch, and I see that others are beginning to own up. Buster Keaton was often cited as his superior, which he was, but his gifts owed more to Shakespearean melancholy than mirth. As a schoolboy, I despised anyone who found certain comics funny: Abbott and Costello, the Three Stooges and the Crazy Gang, who in pairs could amuse, but teamed together were no more than capering old men. 'Alternative comedy' seems to be aimed at those who can't tell sheep-dip from butter, let alone margarine. There used to be a category of comic whose awesome badness gave mediocrity a certain triumphant magnificence. George Formby, King George VI's favourite, was pure margarine. Every music hall could produce a performer far more dismal – Murray and Mooney, Sandy Powell, Clapham and Dwyer – yet these fourth-raters had their place of welcome, like eccentric uncles.

• John Osborne, *Spectator*, 21.5.94

* ☆ *

The other day an actress's small nephew was taken round to her dressing-room after seeing the performance. After some general conversation about the production, he raised a point which obviously had been worrying him.

'I say,' he asked in a rather pregnant tone, 'do you really kiss that man?'

'Well,' said his aunt, 'yes. As a matter of fact, I do.'

A look of revulsion, slightly tinged with incredulity, appeared on her nephew's face.

'Doesn't he *mind*?' he said.

• Celia Johnson, quoted by E C Hodgkin in the *Spectator*, 6.1.96

★ ☆ ★

Friday January 13 [1995]: Death has made some swift, unexpected and sad visitations since Christmas: John Osborne (who could be enchanting), Fanny Cradock and Peter Cook. All regrettable, but the theatre did not begin with *Look Back in Anger*, as we are so frequently instructed; Cradock's cooking appeared, to me, over-elaborate and ill-tempered; and Peter Cook's obituaries seemed to take up more press coverage than would the assassination of the entire Royal Family. I asked Alan Bennett if he could account for it. 'He was a journalist,' he said.

• Alec Guinness, *Sunday Telegraph Review*, 24.12.95

★ ☆ ★

One of the most famous examples of stage fright occurred when Sir Laurence Olivier began suffering from acute anxiety attacks while playing *Othello* in a National Theatre production at the Old Vic in 1965. Aware that he was performing at the height of his powers – weeping for the first time on cue and toying with his audience's emotions – Olivier started agonizing about how he was achieving such superlative performances.

After experiencing difficulties in breathing he whispered to Frank Finlay, who was playing Cassio: 'Don't leave the stage, move down stage where I can see you or I will run – and whatever you do don't look me in the eye, look over my shoulder.'

One of the most widely publicised theatrical collapses of recent years was that of Daniel Day-Lewis in *Hamlet* in September 1989 (again at the National Theatre). Day-Lewis (well known for his intense preparation for every role) found playing the role more than usually disturbing, and, at the height of his distress, experienced hallucinations of his dead father's presence.

'I had the strange sensation I was really talking to my own father,' he said later. 'What he said to me on that night seemed particularly hard to bear.'

Day-Lewis *fils* walked off stage in the middle of the performance and disappeared for the next two years.

• Simon Midgley, *Independent*, 30.12.94

★ ☆ ★

Let's hope Roger Moore's new TV career will be able to solve his identity crisis: 'A young woman approached me recently and asked, "Are you Roger Moore?" I replied, "Sometimes".'

• Peterborough, *Daily Telegraph*, August 1999

★ ☆ ★

'Charles Chaplin in his early days in America was enjoying his riches with becoming modesty,' wrote K Kitchen when Chaplin was at the peak of his career. 'He spent a month in New York before he signed his contract, and it was a dizzy month up and down and across Broadway, dining, wining, play-going and dancing and having the time of his young life, but keeping the bankroll exclusively to himself. For at the age of 26 with an annual income of 670,000 dollars, Chaplin had the finance idea developed to 100 percent efficiency. The only thing he spent on Broadway in a month of gay life was four weeks. Not since Harry Lauder astonished and then amused New York with his Scotch thrift, to use a pleasant word, has Broadway known such a frugal character.'

• David Robinson, *Chaplin*

★ ☆ ★

They Aren't What They Seem

Let's face it, Richard Harris is the man who invented the lost weekend – although, in his case, as he points out, it was often a lost month. On one occasion after a legendary drinking session, he got into the wrong hotel room and climbed into bed with a couple who were not, he admits, of his previous acquaintance. 'What's the big idea, mate?' the outraged husband is said to have yelled as Harris snuggled down between them. 'I don't have one,' Harris replied. 'But if one occurs to you then by all means wake me up.'

• Daphne Lockyer, *The Times* Magazine, 26.5.00

2 Age Is Not To Be Trusted

age

'I'm very uncomfortable living in any world where the Pope is twenty-five years younger than I am.'

• Billy Wilson (87), Film Director, interviewed by Stephen M Sylverman. *The Times* magazine, 10.7.93

★ ☆ ★

From the age of twenty-eight I never did for long anything I didn't want to – except grow old.

• Quentin Crisp, prominent homosexual.

★ ☆ ★

By quitting smoking and joining a gym, I may have extended my life expectancy a bit, but was it worth it? I am starting to have doubts.

Until I stopped smoking, I hadn't realized how many contemplative 10- or 15-minute interludes – Australians call them 'smokos' – are required if you are consuming 40 king-size cigarettes a day, especially if you are at work. Smokos are wonderful. You just sit there and smoke, feeding your addiction, slipping in and out of dream world.

When I was a smoker, I spent hours each day in a fog of bone-idle speculation, speeding to the edge of the universe (if it *has* an edge) between one lethal puff of a full-tar ciggy and the next. No wonder I looked addled.

But you cannot go on like that. Either you die of tobacco, or you stop smoking. Having quit, however, I find that my reactivated brain parts, far from being interested in 1-million-year time-frames, are obsessed only with the next two decades, and with ageing and death. *My* ageing and death. *Their* ageing and death.

Until I quit smoking and joined a gym, I never thought about ageing. Now I think of little else. I have become acutely sensitive to the many changes, physical or otherwise, that ageing entails. As my brain cells constantly remind me, quoting Plato: 'Old age does not come alone.'

Until I quit smoking, I read a lot of science books, especially ones that dealt with mankind's future. One of the books I enjoyed most last year, for example, was Freeman Dyson's *Imagined Worlds*, in which the famed Princeton scientist speculated on the likely evolution of humanity over the next 10, 100, 1,000, 10,000, 100,000 and 1 million years. (Beyond 1 million years, he says, we won't be human any more.)

• *Financial Times*, 2.1.99

★ ☆ ★

'What do you reckon is the best thing about getting older?'

'Not being young.'

'Do you not miss being young?'

'No, not at all. No – I wish I'd been older, earlier. If I'd been older younger, I could have been older longer.'

• Peter O'Toole, winner, Oldie of the Year 2000, interviewed in a taxi by Matt Cain on *Night Life*, ITV, 21.4.00

★ ☆ ★

Last week the movers and shakers of Hollywood were busy affecting moral outrage about the news that Riley Weston, a

Hollywood actress and writer, is not the 19-year-old cutie she has claimed to be, but – *quelle horreur* – an ancient hag of 32. Ms Weston (née Kimberlee Kramer) has been acting on network television for almost a decade but in recent years she has found it increasingly difficult to get auditions; casting directors deemed her too old. Being a can-do girl, she responded to the problem by changing her name, editing out the older credits on her CV and lopping 13 years of her age.

The results were good. In short order, she got a part on *Felicity* and a writing job on the show, which in turn led to a three-year, $300,000 contract to write shows for Touchstone Television. This summer, after *Entertainment Weekly* had with unwitting irony named Weston one of the 200 'most creative people in entertainment', the television show *Entertainment Tonight* decided to do a feature on her. The intention was to celebrate the talent of a teenage phenomenon, but early on in the research some troubling inconsistencies regarding Weston's alleged age emerged. Soon the gig was up.

Maddeningly, Weston has been abjectly apologetic about her pretence. She has been at particular pains to point out that although she pretended to be younger in order to secure acting jobs, she never intended her faux-youth to help advance her writing career.

It's not at all clear to me why pretending to be younger than you are is more morally reprehensible when you're trying to be a writer than when you're trying to be a television babe. In both cases, the burden of moral embarrassment is not on the pretender, but on the system that fetishes youth. The Weston case is salutary in so far as it points up the fact that all workers in the Hollywood system – even writers, who you might reasonably expect to be prized for their experience – feel the pressure of youth-mania. Over the years, I have met no fewer than five male writers who tinted their hair in order that their greying temples would not repulse whiz-kid studio executives. One female writer I know has been 29 for at least half a decade.

• Zoe Heller, *Sunday Times*, 25.10.98

★ ☆ ★

I met Peter Ustinov on a Monday morning. The previous day's papers had revealed that his latest novel, *Monsieur Renée*, was number nine in the hardback bestseller lists. I reminded him of a play he had written in 1962 called *Photo-Finish*, in which the protagonist (whom he played) was an 80-year-old man, looking back at his life at 20, 40 and 60. At the time, the 41-year-old Ustinov had said, 'If I live to be 80 I see myself as somebody full of wisdom, probably not being taken notice of by anybody, and probably quite content.' So how did the reality of his age match up to the way he had anticipated it? 'I've still got two years to go,' he pointed out, then added, 'I feel I can talk with more authority, especially when I say, "I don't know".'

• David Thomas, *Independent*, 28.7.99

★ ☆ ★

A man of forty today has nothing to worry him but falling hair, inability to button up the top button on his trousers, failing vision, shortness of breath, a tendency of collars to shut off all breathing and a general sense of giddiness when the matter of rent is brought up.

• Robert Benchley

★ ☆ ★

Middle age is when you're sitting at home on a Saturday night and the telephone rings and you hope it isn't for you.

• Anon

★ ☆ ★

One of the chief consolations of middle age is looking at a photograph of the girl you didn't marry.

• Anon

* ☆ *

Visiting George Bernard Shaw shortly after his ninetieth birthday, the American comedian Danny Kaye intending to compliment the great playwright said, 'You're a young-looking ninety.' 'Nonsense,' replied Shaw. 'I look exactly like a man of ninety should look. Everyone else looks older because of the dissolute lives they lead.'

• *Faber Book of Anecdotes*, edited by Clifton Fadiman

Danny Kaye

3 To Be Cherished And Eaten

animals

Today I heard a man say to his parrot 'roll over' and the parrot rolled over. This set me thinking: what would be the first thing you would do if you wanted to make a parrot roll over?

Short of rolling it over yourself. I can understand possibly teaching a parrot to speak, but how would you approach the problem of making it roll over? Would you go right up to it and say 'roll over' and then wait? I don't quite see the common ground that one could get on with a parrot as a starter...

There must be some initial move that has to be made and I am glad that I am not the one who has to make it...

Oh well, I have got better things to do than to worry about breaking the ice with a parrot, but right now I can't think what they are.

• Robert Benchley, quoted in the *Observer*, 26.12.99

★ ☆ ★

One of British comedian Tommy Cooper's jokes told of a white hunter about to topple an elephant with his rifle when the animal picked up its foot to reveal a splinter. The hunter pulled it out – and then did not have the heart to shoot the beast.

Years later, the hunter went to the circus and was astonished to see an elephant in the ring lifting up its foot. Rushing to greet his long lost friend, the hunter was promptly flattened.

'It was a different elephant,' said Cooper.

• Arnie Wilson, *Financial Times*, 14.11.98

★ ☆ ★

Turkey farmer Ollie Baker is to save 1,200 birds – because they are hiding his pet turkey, Trudy. Baker, of Chichester, West Sussex, hand-reared Trudy. But she escaped and joined the flock, which was ready for Christmas slaughter. 'I spend four hours a day searching for Trudy,' he says. 'I call her name, but they just stare back at me.'

• *Sunday Times*, 20.12.98

★ ☆ ★

Two monkeys have shaken scientific ideas about counting and language by revealing that they can grasp the concept of numbers ranging from one to nine. Studies published today suggest that the ability to count and numerical reasoning is older than language. Arithmetic and language evolved separately, and number skills preceded human speech.

The three-year-old male rhesus monkeys, Rosencrantz and Macduff, have played video games that reveal they can discriminate between as many as nine objects, without training.

The work is the strongest evidence so far of numerical ability in non-human primates, said Prof. Herbert Terrace, of Columbia University, New York, and graduate student co-author, Elizabeth Brannon.

Mathematics is the language that scientists rely on to describe everything in the physical world, from the inner space of elementary particles to the outer space of distant galaxies.

Its importance is underscored by considering how many counting systems have emerged throughout human history.

Prof. Terrace and Ms Brannon believe that thought processes are needed to explain the kind of complex behaviour they are studying and hope to show that human intelligence, like other human attributes, can be traced to animal origins.

Although the monkeys do not think of numbers, there must be some pattern of nerve activity in their brains that corresponds to 'one', 'two' and so on.

'We have ample evidence that animals can think without language,' said Prof. Terrace, who heads Columbia's Primate Cognition Laboratory. 'In our current and previous research, we have shown that animals solved complex problems without help from external cues.'

Ms Brannon said: 'Though monkeys do not recognise the word "two" or the symbol "2", they share with humans the capacity to master simple arithmetic. We don't have direct evidence yet, but it seems likely that these monkeys, and other non-human primates, can count.'

• *Daily Telegraph*, 23.10.98

★ ☆ ★

The present British monarchy is indelibly associated with small yapping dogs that bite, for better or for worse. Katharine MacDonogh, in this austere, scholarly and intriguing book, brilliantly demonstrates that this phenomenon is part of a tradition, if you can call it that, going back centuries. The Stuarts saw nothing ridiculous in off-setting their magnificence with tiny rat-like lapdogs and indeed had them included in official portraits as an indication of their elegant and secure hold on power. Only a nervous, yobby sort of king would need to be seen out with a socking great mastiff. Kaiser Wilhelm II favoured dachshunds whom he encouraged to urinate over courtiers, while Edward VII made everyone's life a misery with a smelly and self-important fox terrier called Caesar. This mundane animal had a collar which bore the legend, 'I am Caesar, the King's dog.' 'It was as if he knew it,' one courtier remarked.

This ostentatious preferment of nasty toy-dogs over humans is a chillingly contemptuous exercise of power. MacDonogh quite explodes the myth that royalty, in their relations with animals, reveal an endearing 'human' side. Indeed the book amounts to a disturbing and even pitiable exposé of their fundamentally warped and bizarre condition. Queen Alexandra's refusal to be parted from a beloved but unfortunately dead pekinese (Queen sobbing over the corpse, ladies-in-waiting hysterical at the smell) is just the tip of the iceberg. Royal women turned to dogs as a consolation for the restrictions and boredom of court life or, if the dog was large and savage, as a means of keeping their husbands out of the bedroom. The constant company of dogs bred in many royals a belief in canine superiority to humans and MacDonogh confirms what many have long suspected – that dog-lovers often harbour the must cynical and brutal feelings about their fellow human-beings. Frederick the Great believed that his greyhound, Biche, was more rational than most people and he was only able to express, in his correspondence, anything approaching human vulnerability when pretending to write as this animal. A few kings went so far as to actually think themselves dogs, but they were mad.

- Thomas Blaikie, reviewing *Reigning Cats and Dogs* by Katharine MacDonogh, *Spectator*, 4.12.99

★ ☆ ★

Chinese pandas are to be given Viagra in the latest attempt to save the species from extinction. According to an article in the *Beijing Youth Daily*: 'The male panda can only mate for 10 to 20 seconds at a time. With Viagra, the male could mate for up to 20 minutes.'

• This Life, *Sunday Times*, 16.4.00

★ ☆ ★

Actors are not the only ones to suffer from stage nerves. In October last year, a first night revival of Mozart's *Mitridate*, at the Royal Opera House in Covent Garden in central London, was stopped mid performance when Jesse, a buzzard, became so agitated during an aria by the soprano Luba Orgonasova that she repeatedly tried to fly away before keeling off her perch. All that the audience could see was a solitary talon tied to a branch and a cloud of feathers cascading to earth.

The creature's squawking drowned out the sound of hecklers until the end of the aria when an indignant man stood up and yelled: 'Free the bird, you bastards!' The performance was eventually halted to allow Jesse's handler to retrieve her.

A spokesman for the Royal Opera House later said that the bird was suffering from stage fright in the same way that singers got frogs in their throats. 'Apparently when buzzards become distressed they play dead and fall off their perches.'

• Simon Midgley, *Independent*, 30.12.94

★ ☆ ★

The Americans have a Hollywood Oscar called a Patsy, which is awarded annually to the animal within the best screen performance. The awards are made in much the same sort of ceremonial accorded to the human Oscar awards. The winner is announced by a man in a dinner jacket who takes the star name out of a sealed envelope and the winner then acknowledges its victory with a cute sort of 'woof' and comes bounding towards the platform where a woman in a flowing scarlet gown formally awards it the Gold Patsy.

This year's canine star – now a member of the Hall of Fame which houses Rin Tin Tin and Lassie – is a terrier called Benji whose last picture made 12 million dollars in America alone. In Bangkok they have a picture of his head four storeys high and in Greece hotel staff kept asking for his room number. His main rival is Arf, a sandy haired airedale who was a mongrel that made good in a musical called *Little Orphan Annie*. Now that he is a big star, Arf gives hundreds of autographs a day with an ink pad and his right front paw.

• Roderich Gilchrist, *Daily Mail*, July 1977

★ ☆ ★

An elephant looked down on a mouse and said, 'Goodness, you're very small.' To which the mouse replied, 'I haven't been very well lately.'

★ ☆ ★

Among the tales about himself that Peter Langan, the London restaurateur, did not deny was that of the cockroach which a distraught customer had found in the ladies' room. 'Madam,' he exclaimed after studying it closely, 'that cockroach is *dead*; all ours are alive.' He then apparently swallowed it, washing it down decorously with a glass of vintage Krug.

• *Daily Telegraph Book of Obituaries*, edited by Hugh Massingberd

4 What You Can Get Away With

art and artists

The real Toulouse-Lautrec is somewhat at odds with the little man found in most books and films – José Ferrer toddling about on his knees in *Moulin Rouge*, perpetrating the myth of the hard-drinking *roué*, the fallen aristocrat who divided his time between bar and brothel, supposedly the two primary subjects of his art. With Lautrec, I was dealing with someone who needed to be built up.

Here was no drunken hedonist, no bleary-eyed ogler of can-can dancers and street-walkers. The real Lautrec can be found wherever the radical and dangerous were being fomented. He helped design the sets for the first production of Jarry's *Ubu Roi*, the most revolutionary theatrical event of the 19th century, and he worked for the anarcho-literary magazine *La Revue Blanche*. This other Lautrec found his friends and principal subjects among what were then called '*less femmes nouvelles*', women who were making lives and careers independently of men – an analysis of his paintings reveals that most were, at least temporarily, lesbian, preferring the freedom this offered to the restrictions of marriage, a fact that his friends, especially his dealer Maurice Joyent, went to considerable lengths to disguise.

Stripping away the veils that have obscured Lautrec has been very satisfying. The artist that emerges is a multi-faceted genius at the bitter heart of *fin-de-siècle* life, an unflinching observer of a society giddy with change but unsure of its bearings – not unlike our own as we wait for this century to end.

• David Sweetman, *Independent*, 26.10.99

★ ☆ ★

The history of art is littered with examples of great artists who, even when looked at through the rosiest spectacles in Manhattan, could not be described as 'excellent persons'. Caravaggio murdered a youth after a tennis game and spent most of his life on the run, but this didn't stop him from creating some of the most effective and moving religious art ever produced. Toulouse-Lautrec swayed drunkenly from brothel to brothel. Gauguin deserted his wife and children before taking up with a secession of pre-pubescent Polynesian girls and giving them syphilis.

Just when, I wonder, did the duties of an artist include setting the rest of us an example as thinking, loving, fulfilled human beings? No wonder Modernism failed if a guru-like role was demanded of its practitioners. The gap between fantasy and reality grew as wide as the Atlantic.

• Waldemar Januszczak, *Guardian*, 22.8.84

★ ☆ ★

If Botticelli were alive today, he'd be working for *Vogue*.

★ ☆ ★

Moral indignation was always cartoonist Vicky's (Victor Weisz) stock-in-trade, much more than humour. He greatly resented the pressure on him to be funny. 'A political cartoonist is not a comic artist,' he announced. His first editor, Gerald Barry of the *News Chronicle* disagreed, and sent him on a crash course of English humour: *Alice in Wonderland*, *Punch*, Wisden, Dickens,

Shakespeare, Gilbert and Sullivan – even, or above all, sending him to spend hours and hours of stupefying boredom in the Press Gallery of the House of Commons.

Vicky came to acknowledge the idea of the English joke, and frequently used scenes from *Alice* to make some political point or other, but his heart was not in it. He much preferred what he called his 'grim' cartoons, showing death's head to represent war, piles of starved children's corpses to represent the withdrawal of free school milk or whatever.

• Auberon Waugh, reviewing *Vicky* by Russell Davies & Liz Ottaway, *Independent*, 12.12.87

* ☆ *

In 1907 Jacob Epstein, a relatively unknown sculptor at the time, was unexpectedly commissioned to produce eighteen figures for the British Medical Association's new building in the Strand. The appearance of these nude, larger-than-life statues providing a frieze around the building's roof, became the opening shot in the running fight that raged relentlessly between Epstein and the British public for over three decades. Outraged prudery protested that the Strand was no longer a fit place for a father to walk with his daughter or a 'discriminating young man' to take his fiancée. Burly policemen were sent up specially erected scaffolding to study this granite nakedness at close quarters, and one constable, conscious of regulations, summed up his impression by assiduously writing in his notebook the single word 'Rude'.

• *How to be a Celebrity*, by Milton Shulman

Sir Jacob Epstein

5 Books Are Not For Burning

books and authors

Auberon Waugh does not like poets. While applying for a drinks licence for the Academy, his private club in Soho, the Editor of the *Literary Review* was asked by the chairman of the magistrates what kind of people would be patronising the new venue. When Waugh responded that poets were absolutely banned, the JP's face lit up and the licence was issued on the spot.

But why such an extreme literary sanction? 'The reason poets were originally banned from the old Academy was partly that they could talk of nothing but themselves, partly that they never paid for their drinks and partly that all the pretty women fell in love with them.' Bron should rename his club the Dead Poets' Society.

• Diary, *The Times, 9.5.98*

★ ☆ ★

When they met, said James Joyce, 'Proust would only talk about duchesses, while I was more concerned with their chambermaids.'

★ ☆ ★

It Takes All Sorts

Michael Joseph, the publisher, received a telegram from an author who had made an unsolicited submission: 'Must have decision on manuscript as other irons in fire.' Mr Joseph replied: 'Suggest removing irons and inserting manuscript.'

• *Bookseller*, 24.12.99, sent by Paul Robinson

★ ☆ ★

'The greatest living writer of prose', 'the Master', 'the head of my profession', 'akin to Shakespeare', 'a master of the language'... If you had never read Wodehouse and only knew about the world his books inhabit, you might be forgiven for blinking in bewilderment at the praise that has been lavished on a 'mere' comic author by writers such as Compton Mackenzie, Evelyn Waugh, Hilaire Belloc, Bernard Levin and Susan Hill. But once you dive into the soufflé, once you engage with all those miraculous verbal felicities, such adulation begins to make sense.

Example serves better than description. Let me throw up some more random nuggets. Particular to Wodehouse are the transferred epithets: 'I lit a rather pleased cigarette,' or, 'I pronged a moody forkful of eggs and b.' Characteristic, too, are the sublimely hyperbolic similes: 'Roderick Spode. Big chap with a small moustache and the sort of eye that can open an oyster at sixty paces,' or, 'The stationmaster's whiskers are of a Victorian business and give the impression of having been grown under glass.' Here is an example that certainly vindicates my point about his prose working best on the page. Reading this aloud is not much use:

'Sir Jasper Finch-Farrowmere?' said Wilfred. 'ffinch-ffarrowmere,' corrected the visitor, his sensitive ear detecting the capitals.

Then there is a passage such as this, Lord Emsworth musing on his feckless younger son, Freddie Threepwood.

'Unlike the male codfish, which, suddenly finding itself the parent of three million five hundred thousand little codfish, cheerfully resolves to love them all, the British aristocracy is apt to look with a somewhat jaundiced eye on its younger sons.'

If you are immune to such writing, you are fit, to use one of Wodehouse's favourite Shakespearean quotations, only for treasons, stratagems and spoils. You don't analyze such sunlit perfection, you just bask in its warmth and splendour. Like Jeeves, Wodehouse stands alone, and analysis is useless.

• Stephen Fry, *Independent*, 18.1.00

★ ☆ ★

Laurie Lee, author of *Cider With Rosie*, felt he was at his most creative whilst asleep, according to a new biography by Valerie Grove. 'I often make such good jokes asleep I wake myself up laughing,' he said in his Dreams notebook. 'I like dreams... I can talk foreign languages and commit crime. I have put many a bishop in his place and even corrected the Pope on a point of ritual.'

• Brutus, *Daily Express* 2.11.99

★ ☆ ★

With historical hindsight, our literary images of the war come from a handful of poets who experienced the trenches of the Western Front, and wrote about it in the searing language of disillusionment: Owen, Sassoon, Graves, Gurney and Blunden. But, for those who were alive at the time, it wasn't like that at all. Encouraged by the nascent mass media eager to dragoon young men into the trenches, they saw the war, before lengthening casualty lists and the Somme brought second thoughts, in mistily romantic terms of patriotism, self-sacrifice and a cleansing douche to wash away the long corruption of peace with a drenching river of gore.

This was the picture presented right on cue, in a clutch of five sonnets written by the young poet Rupert Brooke in the autumn and winter of 1914 before the terrifying reality had sunk in. The sonnet sequence pushed all the right buttons, such as: patriotism – 'If I should die, think only this of me, / That there's some corner of a foreign field / That is forever England.'

Brooke found the end he had sought and foretold for himself – dying, from septicaemia brought on by an infected insect bite, while *en route* to the blood-soaked beaches of Gallipoli. Fittingly, his death was timed to perfection: he expired on 23 April 1915, St George's Day, and the birth- and death-day of Shakespeare.

'Cometh the hour, cometh the man': Brooke was exactly the figure needed by Britain's rulers to encourage millions of men to emulate his example. Brilliant, beautiful – Yeats called him 'the handsomest young man in England.' Churchill personally orchestrated the PR campaign that lifted the dead poet from life to legend with a grandiloquent tribute in *The Times*: 'He was all that one would wish England's noblest sons to be.' Brooke's complex reality was submerged under a tidal wave of guff that buried the real man under a mountain of well-meant lies. His resurrection from the rubble has taken decades.

For, as his closest friends knew all too well – but weren't telling – the real Rupert Brooke was not the plaster saint of the myth that the politicians and publicists manufactured. Selfish, duplicitous, bisexual, manipulative, misogynist, anti-Semitic, and often downright insane in his obsessive hatreds and paranoia, Brooke was a flawed, if talented, human being with a full flush of faults and neuroses. He was a truly 20th-century schizoid man.

• Nigel Jones, *Independent*, 14.10.99

★ ☆ ★

In a career attended by a great deal of dramatic criticism, one of the most interesting – and indeed acute – critical questions Harold Pinter ever heard was when he was introduced to a young woman and her six-year-old son. The woman looked down at her son and said: 'This man is a very good writer.' The little boy looked at me and then at his mother and said, 'Can he do a W?'

• Harold Pinter, *Various Voices*, 15.3.95

★ ☆ ★

I don't have anything in common with Jews. I don't have anything in common with myself.

• Franz Kafka

★ ☆ ★

Alan Clark said the three foremost ingredients in his diary were lechery, malice and self-pity.

• *Sunday Times*, 18.10.98

★ ☆ ★

There ought to be a correlation between being a genius and being a good man; but that's wishful thinking. George Orwell, Koestler's friend, wrote about Salvador Dali's painting *Dead Mannequin in a Taxi* that the human mind ought to be able to understand that a painting can be good art and morally rotten; so it shouldn't be beyond us to realize that you can be a great painter and a poisonous human being, or a great musician and an infantile lover, or a great President and as rabid as a rabbit. We have ideals, sure – starting with the ideal of courtly love, perhaps; and from whom do we get most of our information on that, via the court of King Arthur? Sir Thomas Malory – who was constantly up on charges of rape. Which gives, now I come to think of it, a whole new meaning to Kennedy's Camelot.

• Katherine Whitehorn, *Guardian*, 22.10.98

★ ☆ ★

Fans of Plum have won a topping victory. Penguin, which is reprinting 40 books by P G Wodehouse, was to depict Bertie Wooster on its covers, wearing a monocle. But when the P G Wodehouse Society discovered the publisher's plans, it became awfully steamed up, complaining that Plum had been far too much of an individual to wear something so clichéd as a monocle. After the fans' intervention, Penguin wisely redesigned its covers.

'The entire thing is a myth,' says Norman Murphy, the Society's top hat. 'It has just sprung up because of the artist Charles Crombie, who drew him in the *Strand* Magazine with a conspicuous monocle between 1919 and 1939. It has no basis in the text at all.'

But John Mortimer, the author and Plum fan, is disappointed to discover the truth: 'I always thought he had a monocle. When I was a young man, I wrote off to Gamages for the eyewear because I wanted to look like him.' Many others who have shared similar desires will feel equally upset by the crushing news.

• Jasper Gerard, *The Times*, 24.11.98

★ ☆ ★

Right-wing American humorist P J O'Rourke was accused of bad taste on Tuesday night after a remark about General Pinochet's victims. 'Pinochet did kill a whole bunch of people,' he declared at a Royal Overseas League meeting to discuss his new book *Eat the Rich*. 'But then again they were bad people.' Most of the audience laughed but one woman complained: 'It's not funny that people died.' 'Ma'am, I want to tell you something about humour. It isn't a nice thing. When a kitten plays with a ball of wool it is only funny when it strangles itself.' My sentiments precisely.

• Brutus, *Daily Express*, 4.12.98

★ ☆ ★

Being shortlisted for the Whitbread First Novel Award must have seemed positively humdrum to the musician-turned novelist Luke Sutherland, compared with winning his parents' approval for his book, *Jellyroll*. 'My parents are quite liberal, but they frown upon swearing,' he tells me. 'The trouble is, much of the language in *Jellyroll* is quite fruity. So when I sent them a copy, I enclosed a bottle of Tippex.' No message was required: the gesture was clear. Even so, Sutherland was caught off-guard when the phone rang the next day. It was his mother. 'I'm not even at the end of chapter two,' she said, 'and I've already run out of Tippex. Please send another bottle.'

• Newman Noggs, *Daily Telegraph*, 14.11.98

★ ☆ ★

Let it be admitted that the first thing I did was look myself up in the index [of Woodrow Wyatt's Journals]. So potential diarists should not include an index. We Establishment figures, the sort of people mentioned in diaries, are very mean. Otherwise we would not rely on people like Lord Wyatt to give us most of our dinners. Nor do we pay for books if we can avoid it. If there were no indexes to diaries, we would have to buy the book, since not to know whether one is mentioned is torture; almost as torturing as being mentioned unflatteringly or inaccurately.

So, in the entry for April 5, 1987 – a time when I was writing *Times* leaders – Lord Wyatt quotes me as telling him that the *Times*' then editor was 'timid'.

Now I would never have said that about that particular editor. It is a mis-quotation. Ignorant, a bully of the weak, a toady of the strong, a man whose rise in life had been at the cost of all courage and dignity; I would have called him all that. But just 'timid'; never! Timid-*brained*, yes; but nothing so timid as just 'timid'.

At which point it occurs to me that I must be the only person mentioned in this diary to complain about being quoted as saying something not malicious *enough*. The entries cover 1985-88. All I can say is that the references to me do not convey the essential envy and lack of generosity which I felt towards plenty of people at the time.

I have dwelt at length on the references to myself, first, because I naturally find them interesting, but secondly because of what might be termed the Diary Issue. The triumph of Alan Clark, and now of Lord Wyatt, mean that more and more diaries will be published. It sometimes seems that half my friends are keeping diaries for publication. Some of them suspect me of being at it myself. Future historians will rely on them, but as history this does not mean that they are reliable. Quotation, as I know in my own case, is selective. The diarists depict themselves as influencing the mighty. We seldom know if the mighty think they are influenced by the diarists.

Because they now live in the diary age, they might just make a Faustian bargain. In return for appearing powerful, rich or glamorous now, they know they must look ridiculous in some diary later. Think of that next time you resent some Mandelson lording it. In due course, the mighty – threatened by diaries – might even start to behave more modestly. Diarists thus carry out the teachings of all of the great religions. They punish hubris, and cast down the mighty from their seats.

• Frank Johnson, *Independent on Sunday*, 1.11.98

★ ☆ ★

My own literary hobby for the end of the Millennium has been to prove that *every* leading writer of English literature before the Second World War may plausibly be regarded as anti-Semitic.

The case was recently made against T S Eliot; it is child's play to label Walter Scott and Dickens as anti-Semites. I have found some cracking passages with which to condemn Trollope. At the moment, though, I am having a bit of trouble with Daisy Ashford.

Daisy Ashford was the nine-year-old author of *The Young Visiters* at the end of the Victorian era. The object of derision in this work is Mr Salteena. My thesis is that Mr Salteena (not an English name) was meant to be Jewish.

He is 'an elderly man of 42', with black and twisty whiskers. He feels isolated in society ('I am not quite a gentleman but you would hardly notice it'). While the heroine Ethel and her beloved Bernard Clark say Christian family prayers at night, Mr Salteena 'was not very addicted to prayers so he marched up to bed.' He is fascinated by money. A sad 19th-century stereotype of a Jewish member of the *nouveaux riches*, surely.

• Christopher Howse, *Daily Telegraph* 1.1.99

* ☆ *

I was struggling over a half-cooked novel when I read that someone had turned up a 60,000-word manuscript that Graham Greene had written years ago and *forgotten about*. I thought briefly about doing away with myself. To me, forgetting having written a book is like forgetting having had heart surgery.

The manuscript was a film treatment which, as always, he had written in the form of a novel. That's something else: I've written film treatments and they read like...well, film treatments. Greene seems unable to put pen to paper without writing like Graham Greene. And then forgetting about it. What hope is there for the rest of us?

• Keith Waterhouse, *The Times*, 6.9.84, a month before Greene's 80th birthday.

★ ☆ ★

In 1967, Brigid Brophy, Michael Levey and Charles Osborne published *Fifty Works of English and American Literature We Could Do Without*. This entertaining piece of iconoclasm argued against the whole concept of the schoolroom 'classic' approach to literature. The 50 works were:

Beowulf; *The York Mystery Plays*; *The Faerie Queen*, Edmund Spenser; *The Alchemist*, Ben Jonson; *Hamlet, Prince of Denmark*, William Shakespeare; *Pilgrim's Progress*, John Bunyan; *Moll Flanders*, Daniel Defoe; *Tom Jones*, Henry Fielding; *Elegy Written in a Country Churchyard*, Thomas Gray; *She Stoops To Conquer*, Oliver Goldsmith; *The School For Scandal*, R B Sheridan; *I Wandered Lonely as a Cloud (The Daffodils)*, William Wordsworth; *The Bride of Lammermoor*, Walter Scott; *The Essays of Elia*, Charles Lamb; *The Confessions of an English Opium Eater*, Thomas De Quincey; *The Dream of Gerontius*, John Henry Newman; *The Scarlet Letter*, Nathaniel Hawthorne; *Aurora Leigh*, Elizabeth Barrett Browning; *The Autocrat of the Breakfast Table*, Oliver Wendell Holmes; *Pickwick Papers*, Charles Dickens; *The Warden*, Anthony Trollope; *Jane Eyre*, Charlotte Brontë; *Wuthering Heights*, Emily Brontë; *Moby Dick* or *The White Whale*, Herman Melville; *Leaves of Grass*, Walt Whitman; *Alice's Adventures in Wonderland*, Lewis Carroll; *Tom Brown's Schooldays*, Thomas Hughes; *The Golden Treasury*, Frances Palgrave; *Lorna Doone*, R D Blackmore; *The Adventures of Huckleberry Finn*, Mark Twain; *Tess of the D'Urbervilles*, Thomas Hardy; *Poems*, Gerard Manley Hopkins; *Esther Waters*, George Moore; *Collected Poems*, A E Housman; *The Hound of Heaven*, Francis Thompson; *Peter Pan*, J M Barrie; *An Habitation Enforced*, Rudyard Kipling; *The History of Mr Polly*,

H G Wells; *The Forsyte Saga*, John Galsworthy; *South Wind*, Norman Douglas; *The Moon and Sixpence* W Somerset Maugham; *To the Lighthouse*, Virginia Woolf; *Lady Chatterley's Lover*, D H Lawrence; *1914 Sonnets*, Rupert Brooke; *Collected Poems*, Edith Sitwell; *Notes on The Waste Land*, T S Eliot; *Point Counter Point*, Aldous Huxley; *The Sound and the Fury*, William Faulkner; *The Silver Chair*, C S Lewis; *A Farewell To Arms*, Ernest Hemingway.

To our delight, the book upset all the right people. Bernard Levin's review called us 'incomparably the three biggest twits In Britain.' When asked in a television interview if we were offended by this, I was able to say that we felt it a compliment, coming as it did from undoubtedly the smallest twit in Britain. All good clean fun, as was the book itself.

Though the essays were not composite jobs, for each of us undertook about a third of the 50, we accepted collective responsibility for all the opinions expressed, and refused to reveal who had written what.

We had, in fact, occasionally been shocked by one another's choices for inclusion. I can still remember the howls of incredulous outrage with which two of us greeted the third's determination to include *Hamlet*. But there are still not horses wild enough to extract from me the name of the collaborator who wrote that 'Hamlet is the posturing, self-pitying, egotistical baby-cum-adolescent in us all, and the play is the prototype of Western literature's most deplorable and most formless form, autobiographical fiction.'

• Charles Osborne, in the week of Brigid Brophy's death, recalling the furore caused by their 'hit list'. *Daily Telegraph*, 12.8.95

★ ☆ ★

Political correctness isn't a modern invention – as witness an exchange of letters between the pioneering women's rights campaigner Marie Stopes and Rudyard Kipling. The letters appear as part of an exhibition of unpublished correspondence and manuscripts, which opens at the University of Sussex in Brighton on Monday.

Stopes wrote to Kipling on May 22, 1925, asking him to change the final line of his most famous poem, *If*.

The poem, written fifteen years previously, thunders to a close with: 'Yours is the Earth and everything that's in it, / And – which is more – you'll be a Man, my son.'

Stopes wondered (the brass neck of her!) whether it wouldn't be improved if the last line read: 'And you will lead the race o'er ground you've won.'

Kipling didn't agree. He scribbled a cursory reply on the bottom of her letter and passed it to his secretary to type up and forward to Stopes.

• Peterborough, *Daily Telegraph*, 29.4.00

★ ☆ ★

Hamlet has come first in a *Sunday Times* readers' poll of this millennium's greatest works of art. This should boost sales of J Dover Wilson's *What Happens in Hamlet*. It was published before the war and, unlike most books so old, has never been out of print. The reason is its title. Nobody knows for sure what *Hamlet* is about. People think the book will tell. It doesn't. It just gives an opinion; a perfectly good one, but an opinion none the less.

It is in that category of books that purport to make easy what we know to be difficult.

If you want to make money from such a book, the title is all. A recent one, which I picked up in New York, is called *Wagner Without Fear*. But the best example of all is by the deceased Tory politician Iain Macleod: *Bridge Is An Easy Game*.

• Frank Johnson, *Daily Telegraph*, 10.4.99

★ ☆ ★

Famous for false modesty, the author Jorge Luis Borges once wrote, 'I would prefer no one to remember me after I'm dead, it would be horrible to think that some day there'll be a street called Jorge Luis Borges, I don't want to be a street, I want to have stopped being Borges, I want Borges to be forgotten.'

• *Guardian*, 18.8.99

★ ☆ ★

Shakespeare, now the people's choice as the greatest Englishman of the Millennium, never became Sir William, nor was Jane Austen ever acclaimed a Dame. I doubt whether either of them would have refused the honour if it had been offered to them, but we cannot be sure.

Kipling, the first English writer to be awarded the Nobel Prize for Literature, declined all honours from the Crown. Virginia Woolf, offered the Companion of Honour, refused it, declaring, 'What damned nonsense it all is!'

When my mother, Vita Sackville-West, was offered the same honour by Attlee, she did not refuse it, but wondered what it was. She asked my father. He said it was splendid, limited to 50 people, and only one degree lower than the Order of Merit. 'But nobody's ever heard of a CH,' she protested. 'Oh, yes they have,' he said, adding as I walked into the room, 'We'll try it out on Nigel. What does CH stand for?' My mind was full of a history of the cavalry I'd been reading. 'Corporal of Horse,' I replied.

• Nigel Nicolson, *Sunday Telegraph*, 10.1.99

★ ☆ ★

I am accounted by some people a good man. How cheap that character is acquired! Pay your debts, don't borrow money, nor twist your kitten's neck off, nor disturb a congregation, your business is done. I know things of myself which would make every friend I have fly from me as of a plague patient.

• Charles Lamb

★ ☆ ★

With a savagery that would make self-flagellating monks pale, France's youngest writers are turning on their bodies, producing a rush of books in which mutilation, degradation and self-disgust amount to an epitaph to sexual liberation.

Two titles, *Viande* and *Apologie de la Viande* – Meat and Apology for Meat – head the procession to an emotional slaughterhouse where the human form is reduced to choice cuts. The trend is being led by young women and homosexual writers.

The sudden outpouring of carnal wretchedness can be attributed to the French publishing industry's peculiar marketing methods: most literary prizes, including the Goncourt are awarded in November, encouraging publishers to release their new works in September.

Some 334 works of fiction, including 75 first novels, are on their way to shops, causing psychoanalysts and literary stylists to worry about the way both body and prose are being put through the mincer.

The re-evaluation of post-1968 joy in sexual freedom started with writers such as Michel Houellebecq and Marie Darrieussecq, whose novels have recently been translated into English. But they seem like old fogeys compared with this year's rising star, Claire Legendre, 20.

In her book *Viande*, the heroine bites off and eats a vital part of her boyfriend, before growing a penis of her own. She then dreams of 'lacerating this organ with great sweeps of a knife, to kill it and wipe out the pain.'

Like most of the Meat Generation, Legendre is a middle-class graduate Parisian whose 50s equivalent would be the romantically disillusioned teenager Françoise Sagan.

One of Legendre's literary rivals is Clotilde Escalle, author of *Herbert Ejaculates*, in which the heroine dreams of her mother cutting open her belly 'to search my intestines for the child I used to be.'

Mutilation is a constant theme for male authors too. In his *Apologie de la Viande*, Régis Cinquart describes the castration of his hero as cutting off 'this dirty little soft gadget, witness of this derisory thing, my virility.'

• Paul Webster, *Guardian*, 3.9.99

★ ☆ ★

There is a phenomenon now, the educated barbarian – who may have been at school for 20 years, has done brilliantly, but who has read nothing, knows no history and is ignorant about anything outside his or her speciality.

It is a bizarre experience, challenging any idea one has held about education, when you are with such a person and have to simplify vocabulary, while you observe blank looks on hearing unfamiliar words like Patagonia, or Goethe. These new barbarians have no idea how ignorant they are, or how they would have been seen by their predecessors. Some of them are teachers. We have to face the fact that there are many who read nothing apart from the books on their syllabus; have never read for pleasure; and cannot pass on an enthusiasm, let alone love, for their subject. Perhaps we may usefully remind them of Carlyle's observation: 'The true education is a good library.'

• Doris Lessing, *Sunday Times*, 15.11.98

6 Children Never Forgive

children

My wife, Drusilla Beyfus, was trying to keep my four-year-old daughter amused on a rainy day when Alexandra was in a particularly uncooperative mood. Drusilla talked her into playing a game of hunting for treasure and on an upturned chair she was rocked pretending to be a ship on the high seas. 'Oh, look,' said my wife, pointing into the distance. 'There's a desert island! Let's see what's on it!'

Alexandra craned forward and peered into the distance. 'Oh yes, I see it. There's a sign on it.'

'Oh,' asked my wife, 'what does the sign say?'

'It says, "No buried treasure here".'

• Milton Shulman

* ☆ *

The danger of open microphones was exemplified by the broadcaster who was reading bedtime stories for kiddies and when he had finished, assuming he couldn't be heard, said: 'And that should keep the little bastards quiet.'

* ☆ *

Lady Antonia Fraser would write her biographies and novels in a hut at the bottom of her garden in Scotland. She wanted isolation from her many children and knew there was a limited distance they would be prepared to run to get her help for trivial matters.

She tested them to discover how far they would like to run and had her hut built ten yards beyond that.

* ☆ *

A baby is a loud noise at one end and no sense of responsibility at the other.
• Ronald Knox.

* ☆ *

Two seven-year-old girls in San Francisco sued the Pacific Bell Company for several million dollars because the company had lured them, by deceptive advertising, into spending 50 cents a call to talk to Santa Claus. They claimed that each time Santa spoke to them he ended his message with the words: 'Call me tomorrow and I'll tell you another story about reindeers.' Assuming that the calls were free, the seven year old, Janis, and her friend phoned 45 times listening to stories that changed on the hour. They are now suing the company claiming they were lured by deception into making the calls.
• News Report, 1985

* ☆ *

The unpredictable reaction of children to a prospective treat organized by their parents was epitomised when a small boy was told he was being taken to the circus again having gone the year before. 'Oh, goodie,' he said. 'All that room under the seats.'

* ☆ *

'We don't know what to make of him,' said the distraught mother of a very badly behaved boy. 'How about a nice rug?' said Tallulah Bankhead, who was asked for her advice.

7 New York, New York

cities and towns

Christmas in New York brings out the Santa Clauses like flies. Go into any store, and there is a Santa Claus sitting in a chair with children crawling all over him. 'Our humble heroes,' are the words that spring to my lips as I see them, for these stores are always warmly central-heated, and you cannot be a Santa Claus without covering your face with beard and whiskers and padding yourself liberally about the middle.

At the end of a business day these devoted men must feel like Shadrach, Mesach and Abednego, and also probably not unlike King Herod, a Biblical character of whose forthright methods I have heard several of them speak, with admiration.

I interviewed one of them the other day in a drug store whither he had gone in his brief time off to refresh himself with a small wassail bowl.

'Don't you ever falter?' I asked.

He gave me a look. 'A Santa Claus who faltered,' he replied stiffly, 'would receive short shrift from the rest of the boys. Before you could say "Saks Fifth Avenue" he would find himself in a hollow square of his fellows, being formally stripped of his beard and stomach padding. We are a proud guild, we Santa Clauses, and we brook no weakness. Besides,' he went on, 'though the life of a department Santa Claus is admittedly fraught with peril, he can console himself with the reflection that he is by no means as badly off as the shock troops of the profession. Take the case of a Santa Claus in whose whiskers a child deposits semi-liquefied chewing-gum.'

'Not pleasant,' I said.

'Far from pleasant,' he agreed. 'A man who has had to comb chewing-gum – or for the matter of that almond chocolate – out of the undergrowth at the close of a working day becomes a graver, deeper man. He has seen life.'

• P G Wodehouse, *Punch*, 23.12.53, quoted in the *Financial Times* 24.12.99.

★ ☆ ★

Scene from New York life: a man who was bumped on an underground train and discovered his wallet missing grabbed a suspect as he stepped on to the platform and, although the door closed on his arm and the train started, kept hold until left with a handful of ripped jacket. When he got to his office his wife called to tell him he had left his wallet at home.

• Dermot Purgavie, *Daily Mail*, 2.6.72

★ ☆ ★

In an era in which people eat lunch on the underground and talk on mobile phones in the street, the middle-class ritual of drawing the curtains to mark the end of the day and shut out the world has become a quaint anachronism.

In my bedroom in Brooklyn, I have a very big and uncurtained window that looks on to the back of a row of brownstones and their gardens. This view – particularly in spring, when the trees are in blossom – is one of the few nice things about my flat, and I am loath to obscure it.

New York thrives on voyeurism. The architecture is partly responsible for this. The way Manhattan is built – all those vertical blocks crammed in on each other – the only uninterrupted view that most New Yorkers have from their flats is of one another. And there is something wonderfully compelling about a New York apartment house at night – each of its tiny yellow windows surrendering a different poignant vignette to the darkness: a woman doing yoga, a man watching late-night television, a couple engaged in the elaborate semaphore of an argument.

I once met a man who cheerfully owned up to having bought a powerful telescope for the express purpose of facilitating his voyeuristic viewing pleasure. What he was really searching for, he said, when he scanned the cityscape late at night from his balcony, was raunchy sex scenes. But alas, while he had been privy to any number of angry domestic battles, teary rapprochements and raucous parties, he had never scored the big one.

I told him about the time I was staying at a hotel and looked out of my window one morning to see a young and rather beautiful couple in one of the rooms opposite mine, making passionate love. Embarrassed and oddly dispirited by the sight, I had turned away. 'Oh!' the man cried at this point. 'And you mean to say you didn't look again?'

Actually I did. Later the same day, I twitched the curtain just to check on whether the beautiful couple were still at it. But they had evidently moved on. In their place was a rather older and less perfect twosome. He was slumped, slack-jawed, on the double bed, watching television. She was sitting, hatched-faced, on the sofa, giving herself a pedicure and drinking a Pepsi from the mini-bar. They were a terrifically grim pair. I watched them for hours.

• Zoe Heller, *Daily Telegraph*, 15.4.00

8 Not Only The Naked Need Clothes

clothes

It takes a lot of money to look this cheap.

• Dolly Parton, Country & Western singer

★ ☆ ★

Website of the Week: Ted Brooks, from the Isle of Man, wrote to the *Daily Telegraph* last week to ask if readers could help in his search for missing socks: 'over the past two years I have accumulated 32 odd socks and I know I am not unique in this dilemma.' Mr Brooks, your troubles are over. Log on to the Bureau of Missing Socks (www.jagat.com/joel/socks.html), which offers a sock-hunting service. Key in the details of your single sock and the bureau will try to find a pair.

This comprehensive sock-related site also features sock news ('Seattle girl eats socks'), a guide to sock references in film and a gallery of celebrity socks.

• Stop the Week, *Sunday Times*, 3.1.99

★ ☆ ★

I am a relentless shirt buyer. I own more shirts than the wives of most dictators own high-heeled shoes. And I am still buying. If I have a single wardrobe-associated ambition, it is to possess one – in some cases two – of every shirt there is.

Forget the Great Gatsby. I am not out to impress anyone with what I can afford. I am in the grip of an irresponsible and essentially private obsession. Remember Frank Churchill in *Emma*, who is charged with 'vanity, extravagance, love of change, restlessness of temper', on account of his having hipped up to London to get his hair cut? Well I am the Frank Churchill of shirts. Hampshire to London? Call that extravagance? Call that restlessness of temper? What would Jane Austen have said had she known I'd been half-way round the world on a steam ship to buy a shirt? So maybe you should forget Frank Churchill as well. I am the Brothers Karamazov of shirts, I am the Marquis de Sade, I am the Casanova of the cut-away collar.

And now you want to know if it's true that I once sailed half-way round the world to buy a shirt. Half-true. I did have other matters to attend to, but shirts were high on the agenda. I had heard of this little clapboard store run by Yemeni tribesmen on the seafront in Aden. That was 35 years ago, since which time the political complexion of Aden has undergone radical transformation. Now, you can probably only get a burnous or a jibbah at the Smart Man's Tailoring Company Ltd. But in 1965 they stocked all the Western shirts your heart desired, Royal Oxfords, herringbones, every size, every colour, single or double cuffs, mafiosi collars, bootlace tie thrown in – not that anyone in their right mind would wear a bootlace tie – seven-and-six a touch. Boxed and all. At that price you don't scruple to buy up the shop. Only when the ship was already steaming towards Colombo did I discover my shirts had neither backs nor sides, neither sleeves nor tails, and that what I'd bought were nothing but false cuffs and dickies padded out with cardboard. Nice boxes, though.

What the hell – it's the packaging I'm in it for anyway. Taking a shirt out of its wrapping is always a massive anti-climax. Bound to be. Who wants an unpinned shirt on a limp hanger? It's the immaculacy of the armless presentation that counts. It's that stiff silk tie jutting out as it never can in real life.

But don't get me started on ties. Hear me on ties and you will think that there's something seriously wrong with me.

• Howard Jacobson, Weekend Review, *Independent*, 22.1.00

★ ☆ ★

The pleasure men get from clothes is small, secret and obsessive. A man's suit has more things up its sleeve than David Copperfield. There's the abiding joy of knowing that your pockets have got pockets. One for change in the right-hand jacket pocket, and, if you're lucky, another inside the trouser pocket. Then there's the ticket pocket, and the watch pocket above the fly with a button-down flap that you've never used. There's a guinea pocket, inside breast pockets, one with a tab for your wallet, and separate pockets for pens.

I once had a suit that boasted 16 pockets and a tailor who reprimanded me for putting anything in them because it spoilt the line. When I asked him to find somewhere bespoke to put a mobile phone, a look of autumn thunder passed over his face: 'Oh no, sir, that wouldn't be the thing at all.' He happily made pockets for fob watches, which nobody has, but drew the line at telephones, which nearly everyone has. Then there are the buttons on the cuffs that might actually undo, but only you and God know they're real buttonholes – having them can mysteriously give self-confidence to a man who enters a room of strange (as in unknown) suited men.

My own favourite secret is a half-inch twist of thread stitched behind the lapel buttonhole, which, naturally, has no corresponding button. The hole is purely ceremonial, for carnations, roses and shamrocks. Personally, I'd rather wear a Greenpeace badge than a flower in my buttonhole, but knowing there is a place to put the stalk if I ever did gives me an almost certifiable amount of pleasure.

At the risk of sounding irredeemably twinky, men treat their clothes like mistresses. In public they pretend they're utilitarian, replaceable secretaries, but in private they're a mass of illicit pleasures. The symbolism of secret pockets shouldn't be lost on any of us. Watches peep from under cuffs like shy woodland creatures, cufflinks burrow up sleeves, wallets lie moleishly furtive in the dark.

• A A Gill, *Sunday Times* Magazine, 16.4.00

★ ☆ ★

Sir, I learnt the following travelling on the Tube in 1951–52, at the impressionable age of 13.

Before Queen Anne Boleyn was sacked
She'd got her suitcase ready packed,
And labelled it, in letters large,
'The Bloody Tower, per royal Barge.'
Her friends all praised her *savoir faire*,
Until they missed their underwear.
For Anne, you see, was no one's fool,
There is no substitute for wool!

• Malcolm I Bruce-Radcliffe, letter to *The Times*, 27.3.00

★ ☆ ★

Sir, The wool verse comes in various attractive versions. Ever topical is one by a senior civil servant:

When Ministers begin to grouse
At awkward questions in the House
When politicians face distress

At odd disclosures in the press
We look for stuff of fitting size
For pulling o'er our master's eyes
We then recall the golden rule:
There is no substitute for wool!

• Alfred Goldstein, letter to *The Times*, 27.3.00

★ ☆ ★

Sir, My favourite rhyming wool ad, which I can date precisely to 1960, was:

When Jonah, deep inside the whale
Seemed cheerful, hearty, even hale,
The whale said, visibly annoyed,
'But aren't you cold in that deep void?'
Quoth Jonah, with a careless shrug,
'My woolly gown keeps me quite snug.'
The whale, impressed, told all his school,
'There is no substitute for wool!'

There was quite a cult among students of the time for spotting and memorising the rhymes.

• Joan Glanville, letter to *The Times*, 3.4.00

★ ☆ ★

Sir, Adding to the London Underground's hall of poetry fame I submit the following:

Judge Jeffreys felt extremely hot
Beneath his ermine. 'Hang the lot,'
He cried, although his inclination
Had been to place them on probation.

It Takes All Sorts

If only he had known the balm
Of wool for comfort and for calm
Then mercy might have been the rule;
There is no substitute for wool!

• Ronald F Austen, letter to *The Times*, 8.4.00

★ ☆ ★

Sir, The latest selection of wool ads reminded me that buried away in the recesses of my memory was this:

When Casanova went to town,
He always took his dressing-gown,
His bed-socks and his knitted gloves –
Which mystified his lady loves.
One gentle temptress asked him, 'Why?'
Quoth he, with an experienced sigh,
'Madam, I used to catch all kinds
Of chills through those Venetian blinds,
So learnt this lesson in love's stern school;
There is no substitute for wool!'

• Peter Shorrock, letter to *The Times*, 13.4.00

9 Travel Broadens The Mind

countries and peoples

A man from Charlotte, North Carolina, having purchased a case of very expensive cigars, insured them against, among other things, fire. Within a month, having smoked his entire stockpile, the man filed a claim against the insurance company, stating that the cigars were lost 'in a series of small fires'.

The insurance company refused to pay, citing the obvious reason that the man had consumed the cigars in the normal fashion. The man sued – and won.

In delivering the ruling the judge, agreeing that the claim was frivolous, stated nevertheless that the man held a policy from the company in which it had warranted that the cigars were insurable and also guaranteed that it would insure against fire, without defining what it considered to be 'unacceptable fire', and was obliged to pay the claim. Rather than endure a lengthy and costly appeal process the insurance company accepted the ruling and paid the man $15,000 for the rare cigars he lost in 'the fires'.

After he cashed the cheque, however, the company had him arrested on 24 counts of arson. With his own insurance claim and testimony from the previous case being used against him, the man was convicted of intentionally burning his insured property and sentenced to 24 months in jail and a $24,000 fine.

• From Michsimon@aol.com, *The Times* magazine, 29.4.00

★ ☆ ★

It Takes All Sorts

This document, labelled 'Instructions on using the water-closets at the artillery regiment', was found on a bathroom door in a Russian regiment in 1991 and sent, anonymously, to a weekly newspaper in Moscow.

1 The water-closet should always be kept clean.

2 No garbage, rags, cigarette butts, matches, dirt or food left-overs should be dropped in the urinals and lavatory pans.

3 While using the lavatory pan, do not mount on top of it with your feet, but sit on it as if it were a chair, with all your might, so that the buttock fully and tightly sticks to the wooden seat of the lavatory pan. Keep the trunk of the body straight and apply absolutely no pressure to the legs – rather, slightly lift your feet from the floor, shifting the legs' gravity on to the buttocks, while keeping the hands resting on the corresponding knees...

4 While using the urinal, it is necessary to approach it closely, even to slightly press against it with your knees; you should lean forward, take out entirely the urinating organ, bend it a little downwards and release the urine to the very last drop. Until the urination is finished, do not depart from the urinal or splash the urine on the floor. By adopting this behaviour there is a possibility that the floor around the urinal will be dry.

The regiment's assistant for cleanness management,

Shimankov

• Translated into English by Anna Husarska and Hendrik Hertzberg, quoted in the *Independent* Magazine, 8.5.93

★ ☆ ★

Whodathunkit? Japanese stores now sell a bra that detects incoming missiles.

• Pandora, *Independent*, 29.7.99

★ ☆ ★

An attempt to produce the German equivalent [of *Yes, Prime Minister*] has run into difficulties... Gerhard Schröder is said to be displeased with *How Was I, Doris?*, a six-part television series about German politics, featuring him and his wife... True, the German sense of humour has been suspect in days past. There was that Bairnsfather cartoon of Old Bill looking at a huge hole and being asked by a rookie who had made it. 'Mice!' says Old Bill.

The German reproduction of the joke carried an explanatory foot-note: 'It was not, of course, mice. It was a shell.'

• *Daily Telegraph*, 21.8.99

★ ☆ ★

As far as mobile phones are concerned, the British err on the dreary side of caution, as in one mobile phone. The Italians have three demanding mobiles each, and some have a flak jacket of the finest silk to accommodate them, each phone with a different ring and a different-coloured cover.

At dinner, I discovered from an Italian prince, who clearly thought I was a minnow in life's wine lake of sophistication, that one telephone is for the office, the second for the wife and the third for the mistress. If pressed by the wife, a chap could ring someone at the office to get him to ring back, so that he could say he had to go no, *cara*, and then be able to ring the mistress.

I have never liked mobiles, always perceiving them as instruments of interruption. In Italy, they are instruments in the orchestra of the country's ballroom of romance.

• Victoria Mather, *Daily Telegraph*, 20.4.00

★ ☆ ★

It Takes All Sorts

Americans are a broad-minded people. They'll accept the fact that a person can be an alcoholic, a dope fiend, a wife-beater, and even a newspaperman, but if a man doesn't drive, there is something wrong with him.

• Art Buchwald

★ ☆ ★

France awakens one's eyes to such delights as good food, good wines and bad losers.

★ ☆ ★

Italian doctors have appealed to women patients not to tempt them by wearing provocative dress to the surgery. 'Italian women, please, enough of sexy underwear,' said a report in Turin's *La Stampa* newspaper. 'Enough of exaggerated make-up, aphrodisiacal perfumes and fishnet tights.'

• *The Sunday Times*, 4.6.00

★ ☆ ★

I was rather shocked to hear of the current outbreak of hostilities between Spain and the Philippines. It hasn't amounted to a battle just yet, with rocket-ship helicopters and 'ground troops' and saturation media coverage; for the moment it's only a diplomatic incident; but it might turn really nasty.

Full-scale wars have started over lesser pretexts than this. Did you catch it on the weekend news? The Philippine government has protested through official channels about the launch, in Spanish supermarkets, of a biscuit called a 'Filipino'. They have taken umbrage at the way the identity of this benign and smiling nation has been exploited, and implicitly traduced, in order to market a few million cookies to the lisping bourgeoisie of a southern European kingdom a few thousand miles away.

Nobody quite understands why they should be so upset. Some say it's because the bikkie in question is dark on the outside and creamy in the middle, and that the name suggests a racist slur about people who are secretly, or aspirationally, white; in the same way that 'Oreos' (the name of a kind of sultry custard cream) became an insulting term in the USA, for upwardly mobile black politicians who sought to curry favour with the white voters of Georgia. But Filipinos are not blacks, they're Pacific Asians, so it's hardly the same thing.

More to the point is: how many other insulting biscuits lurk undiscovered in our supermarket shelves? Should the French government complain about the packets of Bourbons routinely sold to impressionable British consumers, so long after the Revolution that guillotined the dynasty's top talent? Will Italy try to ban the sale of Garibaldi biscuits, whose horrible, squashed-fly features so inadequately celebrate the architect of the Risorgimento? Should a delegation of bigwigs from Baltimore complain that their lean and healthy state is insulted by its association with high-calorie chocolate-chip cookies? I fear for the future of Jaffa Cakes, once Israeli anti-biscuit fundamentalists discover that the sacred name of Tel Aviv Jafo is being used to flog chocolate sponges with an orangey bit in the middle? And I sympathise with the Foreign Office. They will have their work cut out this week to mediate in a dozen such disputes, as they sit in Whitehall working into the night, buoyed up only by draughts of tea and plates of (aarrgh! Oh no!) pink Vienna wafers.

• John Walsh, *Independent*, 30.8.99

★ ☆ ★

A cartoon in the *New Yorker* shows two naked female savages in a hut full of human skulls. The caption reads: 'One thing I'll say for him – he's always been a good provider.'

★ ☆ ★

It Takes All Sorts

In the Second World War the Italians were derided for their military achievements having had disastrous campaigns in Europe and North Africa. They were the butt of much derision. In 1944 it was said that the Italians had produced a new plane for parachutists in airborne operations. It was manned by a crew of fifteen – a pilot, a co-pilot, a navigator, a parachutist and eleven men to push him out.

It seems little has changed since then according to a news story in the *Sunday Times*, June 4, 2000. A planeload of elite Italian paratroopers flew to Sweden for a NATO exercise, surprising immigration officers in Kristianstad when they marched through passport control. The mix-up occurred because their Norwegian destination was the similar-sounding Kristiansand. A Swedish official said, 'Their map skills need a brush-up before they attack the wrong country.'

★ ☆ ★

A little bit of history was made at the weekend when Chelsea football club fielded a team consisting entirely of foreign players – the first time in the life of the Premier league or its predecessors that this has happened. The Blues' supporters have known for some time that, with the preponderance of overseas players in the squad, it was a question of when rather than whether it would happen. The problem is working out what, if anything, fielding a team consisting of a Dutchman, a Spaniard, two Frenchmen, a Brazilian, a Uruguayan, a Nigerian, two Italians and a Norwegian might 'mean'.

It is not very many years since Chelsea was one of the most xenophobic of football clubs, with supporters booing foreign players when they came on to the field – even on occasion their own players. All that belongs to history. Chelsea is now, at least on paper, the most cosmopolitan of clubs; manager Gianluca Vialli inspires deep loyalty among fans. Only the location of the club at Stamford Bridge anchors it in history. That is sufficient to ensure that victory with an all-foreign team (like Sunday's 2-1 win over Southampton) somehow reinforces the Chelsea-ishness of it all.

It is curious how Britain, so reluctant to share a single currency with the rest of Europe, has welcomed continental and non-European players to its bosom.

Of course none of this implies that Chelsea's manager is being anything other than totally meritocratic when he chooses the team each week. It is virtually certain that the team's indefatigable captain, Dennis Wise, will soon be back in the first team. But as no more than a prudent insurance policy he might find it sage to change his name by deed poll to Dennis Raisonnable.

• *The Guardian* 28.12.99

★ ☆ ★

Did you hear about the Irish woodworm? They found him in a brick.

10 Crime Doesn't Pay; Law Does

crime and law

Spotted on the back door panel of a white van on the M1 yesterday: 'If this vehicle is being driven well, please dial 999 and report stolen.'

• *Financial Times* 15.10.99

★ ☆ ★

Roger Cook, the reporter who realized that being beaten up makes for watchable television, recalls a death threat from an Ulster paramilitary: 'He started to issue this threat from a callbox – in mid-threat the pips went and he was cut off,' he tells *Limb by Limb* magazine this month. 'Five minutes later he calls back and apologises profusely. He had gone to the corner shop to get more change in order to finish the death threat, which he duly did.'

• Diary, *The Times*, 12.1.00

★ ☆ ★

Three men were on trial in Texas last week accused of conspiring to assassinate President Clinton with a cactus. The three men – members of a group fighting for an independent Texas – planned to infect the cactus thorns with the Aids virus and fire the spikes at the president using a modified cigarette lighter.

• *Sunday Times*, 25.10.98

★ ☆ ★

It Takes All Sorts

Forget leaves on the line or the wrong sort of snow, this has to be the best excuse yet, from delay-plagued Connex South Central. One of its trains was held up on Monday evening. 'We apologise for the five-minute delay at Coulsdon South,' passengers were told. 'This was due to the presence on the train of four drug dealers.'

• City Diary, *The Times*, 17.2.99

⋆ ☆ ⋆

Burglar Frank Gort broke down and sobbed when he was sentenced to seven years in jail, claiming it was his unlucky number. An understanding judge in San Antonio, Texas, took pity and gave him eight years instead.

• *The Week*, 10.10.98

⋆ ☆ ⋆

Borra's talents as a stage pickpocket depended wholly upon his charm, skill and humour to deceive his 'victims' from the audience. Using the beauty and guile of his wife Ilse to distract them, he would deftly relieve them of watches, wallets and other valuables, ties, braces and even reading glasses. Often he would take the glasses from a stooge's face, place them on his own nose and continue a conversation without the victim being aware.

Taking a man's trouser braces was easier in the 1950s than in later years, when more and more people wore belts, and even the great Borra admitted defeat when he tried to perform the same trick in an Arabic country. Traditional dish-dashes are supported by neither braces nor belt.

Borra was, throughout his life, a great practical joker, and it was a sense of fun that permeated his act. He was the only thief who gave back more than he stole, for not only did he return belongings, and give them a lasting memory of stardom in the ring, but at Circus Knie he would also present each stooge with a bottle of spirits as a souvenir of their encounter. Circus Knie also benefited from the revenue supplied by sponsorship from cigarette firms like Kent and Parisiennes, since Borra's act always included some wizardry with blowing cigarette smoke rings.

Borra's passion for practical joking nearly got him the sack from Bertram Mills Circus, however; when he played a joke on his employer, Cyril Mills. Mills later recounted:

'On one occasion he and Ilse were among a dozen of us who went to a country hotel to dine one Sunday evening. When the waiter served cocktails Borra whispered something to him. He knew I had a passion for peanuts and when the waiter returned with them he was asked the time, but his wristwatch had disappeared when the nuts were ordered. When I took a handful of nuts and took the first bite I had to splutter the lot over the floor for Borra had substituted some of his own. The business with the waiter's watch had not been to amuse him only; its real purpose was to take my eye off the peanuts for a second or two. He had spent the whole afternoon drilling holes through peanuts, filling them with cayenne pepper and sealing the ends with butter.'

On another occasion, at a civil reception, Borra stole the Mayor's watch, causing the local Chief Constable to laugh. But the laugh was on him when Borra discovered the mayor's watch in the Chief Constable's pocket. Throughout his tours of England, Borra was able to dupe leading police officers at such functions and eventually became an adviser to Scotland Yard, Interpol and other police agencies of Europe on the art of picking pockets. The police force of Berne, Switzerland, extended to him a particularly unusual privilege, pledging to give him a private cell should he ever be arrested in their jurisdiction.

Borra was born Borislav Milojkowic in Belgrade in 1921, and spent his early years watching for shoplifters and pickpockets in his father's store. From watching their techniques, he became a professional stage magician and pickpocket by the age of 15. In

1938, his big break came in Sarajevo, when his skills came to the notice of the police authorities at a big police congress.

Escaping from Yugoslavia during the Second World War, when he gave troops shows, he made his way to Italy, and offered his services to the British forces, becoming part of the Ensa entertainment corps. He was sent to Austria, where he was reunited with his wife Ilse, whom he had married before war broke out. She was from the family of Kludsky, the most famous name in Czech circus circles. Together they settled in Graz, where they had a farm.

Borra had his own philosophy regarding his art of honest deception: 'Sigmund Freud said that there's a criminal down deep in every person. Perhaps I, too, am a kleptomaniac, but I get a double satisfaction: when I take, I give back, and that makes me happy. When I can do that, I don't have to really steal.'

• D Nevil, Weekend Review, *Independent*, 31.10.98

★ ☆ ★

Apropos of the criminal justice system, I heard a delightful story last weekend. In the 1840s the Ditchley estate was owned by an Irish peer, Lord Dillon. He had invited a few friends to help him cull his partridges, and a good day's sport had ensued. As they returned to the big house for refreshments, the aristocrats encountered a party of yokels who were already well-refreshed. 'Where have you fine fellows been enjoying yourselves?' inquired his Lordship. 'Arr, my Lord,' came the reply, 'us 'ave been over at Little Piddington, watching the 'anging.'

'Christ,' said Lord Dillon, bringing his hand to his face in horror, 'I've got that man's reprieve in my pocket.'

• Bruce Anderson, Diary, *Spectator*, 1.1.00

★ ☆ ★

After this week's reports that a prisoner, Gary Johns, is still on the run from Wormwood Scrubs, a reader has information about the events that preceded the breakout. Shortly beforehand he saw Johns perform in a prison play. The piece was Timberlake Wertenbaker's *Our Country's Good*, which concerns a group of convicts in Australia who are themselves putting on a stage production.

'He had a small part as a vicar,' says my man in the audience. 'His character warned that the play would only cause trouble among the prisoners. Then, sure enough, under cover of rehearsals two of the convicts escaped.'

• Diary, *The Times*, 10.8.95

★ ☆ ★

Jonathan Aitken says that the only good thing about staying with the Queen [being in prison] is the moving. Unlike the outside, once inside you're not burdened with possessions; the physical act of moving is accomplished painlessly and immediately.

All you do is gather your two blankets, two sheets, one pillowcase, the extra pair of trousers, one extra shirt, one piece of underwear and a pair of socks, as well as one toothbrush, razor, soap, shaving cream and tiny wooden mirror, and...presto. One thing is for sure. The worst, which is the first night and the fear of the unknown, are over.

Jonathan was lucky to have a cell of his own. In my time, Pentonville was not only considered the lousiest prison in the land – it was the last one to have slop-out – it was also the most overcrowded. For habitual criminals, a single cell was considered a punishment. When I managed to get mine I was over the moon.

Jonathan has written to his mother that he has acquired an Afro-Caribbean fan club. He helped a fellow prisoner fill in eviction notices and housing benefit forms. Yours truly, ditto. On my second day inside – this was 15 years ago – a large black man by the name of Warren asked me to help him with his appeal. He was illiterate, and was basing his appeal on the fact that none of his six common-law wives could reach an orgasm with anyone else but himself.

Ergo, by keeping him inside, the state was depriving six innocent women of their civil right to have an orgasm. (Warren claimed to be in for fraud, but in reality I suspect it was armed robbery.) I dissuaded him from such an appeal by reminding him that most English judges were queer, and would look upon a straight stud like himself with contempt. 'Yeah, I guess you're right,' said Warren, and that's how my reputation spread that Pentonville had an intellectual in its midst.

• Taki, *Spectator*, 19.6.99

★ ☆ ★

Malaysia's *Straits Times* reports that a new, illegal drug is hitting the streets. According to deputy home minister Ong Ka Ting, quoted in the July 9 edition, this unnamed drug is both cheaper and more dangerous than ecstasy, which in Malaysia is famous for causing 'the head-shaking syndrome'. Ong Ka Ting tells the paper: 'If ecstasy users cannot control the head-shaking after taking the pill, then users of the other [new] psychotropic drug are prone to shake their buttocks non-stop while experiencing it.'

• The Editor magazine, *Guardian*, 23.7.99

★ ☆ ★

The Lord Chief Justice of England recently said that the greater part of his judicial time was spent investigating collisions between propelled vehicles, each on its own side of the road, each sounding its horn and each stationary.

• 1981

★ ☆ ★

Even Thomas Jackson, the judge in the marathon Microsoft monopoly case, dozed off this week – numbed into submission along with the leading attorneys by a mind-blowing mix of legal and technical argument.

First, Microsoft attorney John Warden took 40 winks and then Stephen Houk, lead attorney for 20 states, relaxed a little too much. But instead of calling an adjournment, the judge told a computer joke. A survey had been done, he told the court, to find out whether computers should be referred to as masculine or feminine. Women said computers were definitely masculine; to get their attention you had to turn them on. And as soon as you commit to one, you realize you could have got a better model if only you'd waited a little longer.

The men said computers were most certainly feminine. Even your smallest mistakes are stored in long-term memory. And as soon as you commit to one, you find that you're spending half your pay on accessories. Cue for brief laughter, before eyelids once more descended.

• Observer, *Financial Times*, 19.11.98

11 The Deadly Art

critics

'I would not have believed,' writes Harold Hobson about an actor's performance, 'that words as simple as "I have never been to Birmingham before" could be so heart-rending, or such a revelation of loneliness, as they were when spoken by Miss Blethyn.'

• Harold Hobson, *Sunday Times* quoted in *Private Eye*'s *Second Book of Pseuds*

★ ☆ ★

Before his death, D H Lawrence wrote bitterly of his fellow Englishmen, some of whom turned against him for his eroticism and his promiscuity. 'Curse the blasted, jelly-boned swines, the slimy, the belly-wriggling invertebrates, the miserable, sodding, rotters, the flaming sods, the snivelling, dribbling, dithering pulse-less lot that make up England today.'

• Michael Burke and Andrew Alderson, *Sunday Telegraph*, 4.6.00

★ ☆ ★

God was bored with him.

• Victor Hugo about Napoleon

★ ☆ ★

It Takes All Sorts

My face looks like a wedding cake that has been left out in the rain.

• W H Auden about himself

★ ☆ ★

That old town clerk looking at foreign affairs through the wrong end of a municipal drainpipe.

• Winston Churchill on Chamberlain

★ ☆ ★

Clement Attlee, British Labour Prime Minister, reminds me of nothing so much as a dead fish before it has had time to stiffen.

• George Orwell

★ ☆ ★

Clark Gable's ears made him look like a taxicab with both doors open.

• Anon

★ ☆ ★

Diana Rigg [in the nude in *Abelard and Heloise*] is built like a brick mausoleum with insufficient flying buttresses.

• Simon

★ ☆ ★

Glenda Jackson has a face to launch a thousand dredgers.

★ ☆ ★

Dennis Quilley played the role in high spirit with all the charm and animation of the leg of a billiard table.

• Bernard Levin

★ ☆ ★

Geraldine McEwan [in *Richard II*], powdered white like a clownish, whey-faced doll, simpered, whined and groaned to such effect as the Queen that Edward's homosexuality becomes both understandable and forgivable.

• Milton Shulman

★ ☆ ★

I have always been very fond of theatre critics. I think it so frightfully clever of them to go night after night to the theatre and know so little about it.

• Noël Coward, quoted in the *Sunday Telegraph*, 21.11.99

★ ☆ ★

With Val to see play *Look Back in Anger* by John Osborne, whom I once interviewed on television without being able to get anything out of him. Play quite execrable – woman ironing, man yelling and snivelling, highbrow smut, 'daring' remarks (reading from a Sunday paper; Bishop of…asks us all to rally round and make hydrogen bombs). Endured play up to point where hero and heroine pretended to be squirrels.

• Malcolm Muggeridge, 16 March 1957, quoted in *Independent on Sunday*, 11.10.98

★ ☆ ★

Jackie Mason – once Jacob Maza – is an old-fashioned music-hall entertainer (once he'd done with being a rabbi, he became Social Director at a Catskills hotel, performing complete with yarmulka). He likes observational one-liners, and being oldish (64), a little plump and jowly, short, grey when not dyed, and very Jewish, he's in a position to be rude to whomever he wants. His catchphrase, 'and I say this with the greatest respect,' is used as a preface to every insult. 'Puerto Ricans? Now I say this with the greatest respect...'

His Jewish material is less whiney than Woody Allen's, but still full of self-deprecation. He's fond of doing impressions of Jews struggling with the physical world: lots of hand-to-forehead angst about house-buying, computers, call-waiting or in-flight turbulence, the Jews always turning to Gentiles for explanations. The interval, he explains, is to give the Jews in the audience an opportunity to argue about his age, discuss if he's any good ('he's good', 'he's not good'), and to tell each other about their headaches. And there are streams of surreal, meandering monologues: wondering why kids never show you pictures of their grandparents – 'And here's Grandpa, putting his dentures in a glass.'

If it goes quiet, Mason smirks and stares at someone in the front row: 'These are all jokes, stupid. Why does no Jewish man ever laugh without looking at his wife?'

• Tobias Jones, *Independent on Sunday*, 15.11.98

★ ☆ ★

The design, and the appallingly intrusive percussive sound effects which make ancient Egypt sound as though it is suffering from a disastrous crisis in its plumbing system certainly don't help.'

• Charles Spencer, reviewing *Antony and Cleopatra* at the Olivier Theatre, *Daily Telegraph*, 21.10.98

★ ☆ ★

As Antony, grizzled Alan Rickman's delivery is a disaster, almost devoid of recognizable landmarks. In whole speeches there might be not one intelligible line, and only a dozen or so words. Perhaps it was the droopy moustache – or perhaps the kazoo he seemed to have concealed in it – a strange nasal drone on one note often protruded through his fudgy consonants and warped vowels.'

- David Murray, reviewing *Antony and Cleopatra* at the Olivier Theatre, *Financial Times*, 22.10.98

★ ☆ ★

A master of the close-up, voice-over and reaction shot, Alan Rickman is stumped in the Olivier: unable to find the energy to spin iambic pentameters in front of 1,000 people. His nasal slur rises and falls mainly in volume. I had one of the best seats in the Olivier. I had just read the play. And I was looking for the subtitles.

- Robert Butler, reviewing *Antony and Cleopatra* at the Olivier, *Independent*, 25.10.98

★ ☆ ★

The joy of this programme was naturally, nakedly, the old guard, who, in letting their bits out, dressed themselves in the full panoply of a Surrey golf club, with all its pertinent rules, subsections and points of order. They made nudity utterly English by being pooterishly pompous and as small-minded as possible – and doing it while stark naked. The attraction of public nudity in the company of hideous octogenarian strangers in a wood in Hertfordshire has always eluded me. I can see the point in St Bart's or St Tropez, alongside resting supermodels and pert starlets, but then that's not true naturism, that's just being on holiday with the Italian paparazzi. Call me erotically repressed, but it doesn't seem to be quite the same thing round a paddling pool in Borehamwood.

It Takes All Sorts

Both New and Old nudists banged on about the freedom that nakedness brings. But freedom to do what, the programme failed to ask. Hardly the freedom to walk into a Newcastle pub and say: 'Make mine a large one, darling,' nor yet the freedom to go clothes shopping on Bond Street – 'Could you put that in a bag, I'll wear it later in the privacy of my own home to see if it fits.' It seems that the only freedom available to nudists is to sit and shiver next to a couple of wooden huts on wasteland, surrounded by high fences and barbed wire. So perhaps it was after all an idea brought back from Germany, Stalagluft 49.

• A A Gill, *Sunday Times*, 29.11.98, reviewing *Acting Natural*, Channel 4 (23.11.98)

★ ☆ ★

Wagner's music is better than it sounds.

• Mark Twain

★ ☆ ★

Every time we hear a disc jockey play the top 40 tunes, we get the shakes thinking what the bottom 40 must sound like.

• Anon

★ ☆ ★

I've just bought a great double CD for only £9.99 in the HMV sale. It's called Chegger's Choice, and it's Keith Chegwin's selection of 40 of the worst pop records ever made – many of them former number one hits. Remember Chirpy Chirpy Cheep Cheep? Or Billy, Don't Be a Hero, Agadoo, and Son of My Father?

There are basically two kinds of utterly rotten record – those with pretensions and those without. Among the classic, awful, fully orchestrated errors, those great vinyl cowpats, are

MacArthur Park, Neil Diamond's I Am I Said, and my own personal all-time hate, Where Do You Go To, My Lovely? ('Yes you do, ha ha ha!')

But a lot of novelty rubbish has considerable charm. Jonathan King made many of the best of the all time horrors, including Johnny Reggae ('e's a really taste geezer'), nominally by the Piglets, and Leap Up And Down (Wave Your Knickers in the Air) allegedly by St Cecilia. I remember many happy times – well, two – bopping to that at parties where I had imbibed not wisely but too well.

• Simon Hoggart, *Guardian*, 15.1.00

★ ☆ ★

Of all the noises, I think music the least disagreeable.

• Samuel Johnson

★ ☆ ★

At last the call came which every journalist in the Beaverbrook Group coveted and feared. I was summoned to Beaverbrook's penthouse flat in Arlington House, just behind the Ritz Hotel, on April 5, 1948. April was a significant month for Beaverbrook for that was the date which entitled him to return to Britain and not have to bear the punitive tax rates which for him would have been ninety percent at the top rate. He was standing at a podium in front of a large glass window which had a sparkling view of Green Park and in the distance the roundabout hurly-burly of Hyde Park Corner.

His face opened into a welcoming smile as he shook my hand and led me to one of the many armchairs scattered in the large living-room. His wide mouth and softly simian appearance were already familiar to me through the many photographs I had seen of him. I had already equipped myself with details of his personal history – son of an impoverished New Brunswick preacher who became a multi-millionaire by thirty, Minister of Aircraft Production in Churchill's war cabinet, owner of the *Daily* and *Sunday Express* and the *Evening Standard* – he was probably the most successful and most controversial tycoon in the history of Fleet Street. He looked large even though he was only about five foot nine inches tall. He was already a legend and if I had never seen him again I would have thought it a privilege that I had once been in such close proximity to him.

He signalled me to take the chair opposite him and asked me about my Toronto background. Then he switched to *Defeat in the West* and asked me about my views of the senior German generals and whether or not I thought a Second Front could have been undertaken in 1943 instead of 1944. He had read some of the interviews I had done for the *Standard* and had enjoyed them, particularly the ones on Danny Kaye and Mae West.

'Now, Mr Shulman, what do you know about films?' he suddenly asked me, for no particular reason.

'Not very much,' I replied, not knowing what he expected me to say.

'Do you go to them?'

'Not very often. About once or twice a month, I would guess.'

'Good!' said Beaverbrook, seemingly having got the answers he had been waiting for. He stood up and walked to his podium and began to scribble on a sheet of paper. 'Just the man we want. A fresh mind on the subject of films. Starting in two weeks time you will be the film critic of the *Evening Standard* and your salary will be raised by £10 a week.'

He didn't ask me if I wanted the job. I listened to him somewhat stunned as he talked into his dictaphone. 'Mr Millar,' he said to his secretary, 'tell Mr Gunn that Mr Shulman will be taking Margaret Lane's place as film critic of the *Standard*. She is going in two weeks and she will show him what to do. He will be getting £10 more a week.'

Having settled my future without hearing a word from me, he started to walk me to the door.

'Margaret Lane is giving up the job,' he said, 'and she will take you to next week's film press shows. Mr Gunn will organize it.'

He shook my hand and with a twist of his wrist indicated by his strong handshake that he expected me to leave.

'I will be in touch with you soon,' he said. 'Being film critic of the *Evening Standard* is a very important job. All the film companies will want you to say nice things about their pictures. They will try to bribe you with money, liquor and women. Good-bye.'

I wandered into Piccadilly bemused at what had happened to me. What did I know about films? How long could I possibly keep that job? But his last words were still echoing in my ears. Money, liquor and women! Even if it lasts for only a short time, I consoled myself, this is easily the best job I've ever been offered. And ten pounds extra a week as well! My head was in the clouds and my feet barely touched the ground.

'Soon' turned out to be the very next day. I was told to go to Victoria Station and take a train to Leatherhead where I would be picked up by Lord Beaverbrook's chauffeur at 12.30. I would be having lunch with His Lordship at Cherkley, his country home. To those of us who became the object of Beaverbrook's whim, a peremptory summons to Cherkley or Arlington House always set up a tingling sensation of expectation and unease as we speculated about what fresh test we were likely to be asked to meet.

Cherkley was a nineteenth-century country house with a large, rolling lawn, a splendid view and boring furniture. His butler, Nockles, met me at the door and Beaverbrook and I dined in solitary splendour in his ample dining-room. My only contribution to the conversation was a few answers about my work in MI14(b), which he knew little about. He then went on to tell me a few anecdotes about Bonar Law, a Canadian who had become British Prime Minister and for whom he had been a personal assistant before the First World War. But he was particularly keen on talking about Lord Louis Mountbatten who he blamed for Dieppe and other military disasters.

Throughout the lunch, not a word had been said about my new job as a film critic. Suddenly, as if remembering why he had asked to see me, he rose from the table and led me into a small private cinema which he had had installed at Cherkley. It was equipped with comfortable armchairs – about twelve of them – which were located on two levels of the room. When we were seated, Beaverbrook called out to his butler, 'Nockles, put on two reels of *The Big Clock*.'

The lights went down and hardly were the opening titles finished when I could hear gently snoring sounds beside me. Beaverbrook was asleep. Since a reel was about ten minutes long, the screen suddenly went blank twenty minutes later and the lights in the cinema went up. This awakened Beaverbrook.

Up to this point, the preliminaries of the plot of *The Big Clock* had only just begun to unfold. The story was set in a newspaper office and I had been paying only casual interest to what was going on amongst the characters.

'Who killed her?' were Beaverbrook's first words, still shaking himself out of his short nap.

'Who killed who, Lord Beaverbrook?' I asked. There had been no signs of any such impending violence in the two reels I had seen.

'The blonde. Who killed the blonde?'

'I'm sorry, sir,' I said, 'but I haven't seen any blonde. She hasn't turned up yet in the plot.'

There was a slight pause while he digested this information.

'Well, if there had been a blonde who do you think would have killed her?'

I decided not to guess because I had no idea what the characters were up to. I said I didn't know. I had the feeling I had let him down.

'Ah, Laughton did it. Laughton killed her.'

Since Charles Laughton had not yet made an appearance in those first two reels, it was not altogether surprising that I had not spotted him as a chief suspect.

Beaverbrook rose from his chair. 'Now if you were writing a review of *The Big Clock* what would you say about it?'

'It has lots of suspense,' I said, groping frantically for the appropriate adjectives I had associated with film criticism.

'Yaas. What else?'

'It's very tense.'

'Yaas. What else?'

'It's taut.' I wasn't sure what that meant but I thought it sounded knowledgeable.

'Taut. Ah, yaas.' We had now reached the exit door of the viewing room. 'All right now. You go home and write me two hundred words about *The Big Clock*. And let me see it tomorrow afternoon.'

I was ushered into a chauffeur-driven car and taken to Leatherhead Station. I was too pusillanimous to admit to my proprietor that he had given me an impossible job. All the way back to London I contemplated the fact that my career as a film critic was about to be the shortest in Fleet Street annals. I knew nothing about the story, the stars, the direction of *The Big Clock*. I would have to admit the next day that I could not write the review that was expected. Nor could I possibly bluff my way through it.

Suddenly it occurred to me that if Beaverbrook had a print of the film, there must be other prints in London. Perhaps if I phoned Paramount, who produced the picture, and told them of my plight, they might arrange a screening for me the next morning. Better still, I thought, the movie might be showing somewhere in London. Scanning the *Evening Standard* entertainment advertisements, I found it. It was at the Plaza Cinema in Lower Regent Street, and at 10 o'clock the next day I was at the first showing, practically alone, seeing *The Big Clock* for the first time. The two hundred words were duly written.

• Milton Shulman

12 Money Talks And Says Goodbye

economics and money

Like many people who write about money, Karl Marx was no good at managing it. One day he saw a tobacconist in Holborn advertising cheap and very inferior cigars with the slogan 'The more you smoke, the more you save'. He told his friends that he would save one and sixpence per box by buying this new brand, and that if he smoked enough of them he might one day be able to live on his 'savings'. But, as Francis Wheen writes in his biography of Marx, 'the theory was tested with such lung-rasping commitment that eventually the family doctor had to intervene, ordering the wheezing patient to find some other way of enriching himself.'

• Noel Malcolm, reviewing Francis Wheen's biography of Karl Marx, *Sunday Telegraph* 26.8.99

★ ☆ ★

There are those who believe business all comes down to sex. Prominent among such adherents are certain behavioural psychologists who think the principal motivator for entrepreneurs is the achievement of reproductive success. They study the animal kingdom and draw analogies between the activities of the rich and the mating rituals of lesser creatures.

Such research should not be dismissed as farcical, although a hoary old joke might be in order here. It concerns the 70-year-old who had grafted long and hard to become a multi-millionaire.

He then promptly married a beautiful 20-year-old. His friend was very impressed and asked how he ensnared such a lovely young wife.

'It was easy,' said the old rogue. 'I told her I was 95.'

Luke Johnson, *Sunday Telegraph*, 9.1.00

★ ☆ ★

I spent a lot of my money on booze, birds and fast cars. The rest I just squandered.

• George Best, quoted by Stephen Pollard, *Daily Express*, 10.2.99

★ ☆ ★

My brother down in Texas
Can't even write his name.
He signs his cheques with X's
But they cash them just the same.

• Anon

★ ☆ ★

If you want to know what God thinks of money, just look at those he gives it to.

★ ☆ ★

True you can't take it with you, but that's not the place where it comes in handy.

• Brendan Francis

★ ☆ ★

A bank is a place that will lend you money if you can prove you don't need it.

• Anon

★ ☆ ★

Anyone who lives within his means suffers from a lack of imagination.

• Anon

★ ☆ ★

Money can't buy friends but you can get a better class of enemy.

• Spike Milligan, 1981

13 The English Art Is Muddling Through

England and the English

Think of what our future stands for
Books from Boots and country lanes
Free speech, free passes, class distinction,
Democracy and proper drains.

• John Betjeman, *In Westminster Abbey*, 1940

★ ☆ ★

Old instincts die hard in London clubland. After misleading reports earlier this month suggesting that the Government would force all-male private clubs to admit women, the London Sketch club is making its own, idiosyncratic gesture: women have been told that they can join the 100-strong, men-only contingent of arty eccentrics – if they 'agree to pose naked'.

The Sketch Club is an odd place. Formed on April Fool's Day 1898, and boasting alumni including Robert Baden-Powell and Heath Robinson, the reclusive body of professional and hobby artists gathers in a Chelsea den to paint live models. After one of the silent, two-hour sessions – broken only by the sound of scratching pencils and the grunts of aged members – the artists and models gather over a glass to assess their work.

'A member told me I could join, but only if I posed for them in the nude,' says a blushing female artist. 'I don't think they were joking. It rather put me off. I think they are a bit barmy.'

★ ☆ ★

To succeed pre-eminently in English public life it is necessary to conform either to the popular image of a bookie or of a clergyman.

• Malcolm Muggeridge, quoted by Ian Hislop, *Sunday Telegraph* Magazine 1.1.99

★ ☆ ★

A driver lost near Leeds stops to ask a local the way. 'Excuse me, do you know the Bradford turn-off?' Pause. 'I should do. I married her.'

• George Melly quoted in Pandora, *Independent*, 20.1.00

★ ☆ ★

T S Eliot on the national culture: All the characteristics and activities of a people; Derby Day, Henley Regatta, Cowes, 12 August, a Cup Final, the dog races, the pin-table, the dart board, Wensleydale cheese, boiled cabbage cut into sections; beetroot in vinegar, nineteenth-century Gothic churches and the music of Elgar.

• *Observer*, 11.10.98

★ ☆ ★

To talk of a 'British character' never really made sense. Mostly, when great cartoonists or film-makers or writers pictured the British, they meant the English. And not all the English, either, but mainly the middle-class English of the Home Counties.

In the 18th century, after all, the British were thought of as rowdy, coarse and violent. The Gaels have always been tinged with wildness. And what about the common people of Liverpool, Newcastle or Bristol? Do you think of irony or hypocrisy as being typical there? Has 'le fair play' really been the main story of East London and Essex? Do the Moslem inhabitants of Birmingham have a 'typically British' sense of humour?

No, each time. 'Britishness' is a reflecting glass ball. We can simply take whatever values we most cherish or hate and claim them as typical. I value a down-to-earth suspicion of windy ideas; political stroppiness; the democratic spirit; a well-developed sense of the ridiculous and an instinct for fairness. I would argue that Britishness means all that. Deep down, though, I know it's personal propaganda. It doesn't have much to do with the original values of the new British state – anti-Catholic bigotry and a talent for warfare. Does anyone wish that it did?

• Andrew Marr, *Daily Express*, 7.10.98

★ ☆ ★

Experts have long tried to put their finger on exactly what rings so embarrassingly false about our national anthem. Purcell's reworked version of an earlier tune clearly lacks the elan of France's Marseillaise, the thumping dignity of Haydn's German work (calling it Deutschland Über Alles is now *verboten*), or even the rolling sonorous quality of Russia's anthem. A number of composers, including Elgar and Benjamin Britten, have tried to pep it up, with limited success.

The words sound as if they were written in a military emergency, which they were of course, as George II's troops went north in 1745 to stop Bonnie Prince Charlie. Although the reference to crushing 'rebellious Scots' was excised, the second verse still exhorts God to confound our enemies' politics and frustrate their knavish tricks. Shorn of context, the words sound arch and inappropriate – or would if anyone could remember them.

What distinguishes our national anthem from others is that it is a personalised veneration and not a people's anthem, which Land of Hope and Glory clearly is. Times change and it would be a kindness if the song of Empire was bottled in mothballs and consigned to history.

• News Review, *Sunday Times*, 18.10.98

★ ☆ ★

Every branch of the arts, humanities and sciences gained luminaries. Others will have their little lists; here are mine. In history, Namier and Elton; in philosophy, Wittgenstein and Popper; in economics, Hayek and Bauer on the Right, Kaldor and Balogh on the Left; in the history of ideas and literature, Berlin and Steiner; in sociology, Mannheim and Elias; in psychology, Klein and Eysenck; in music, Menuhin and Brendel, Klemperer and Keller; in art history, Gombrich and Pevsner; in literature, Canetti and Koestler.

The free spirits from unfree Europe also included figures whose role in British society is not easy to define, but who lubricate the mechanism of the metropolitan mind. The publisher Lord Weidenfeld's hospitality and his connections are unique in the pattern of London life; the flavour of his parties has always been international but firmly Anglophile.

That cosmopolitan patriotism permeated the circles of intellectuals around journals such as David Astor's *Observer* or Melvin Lasky's *Encounter*; the cloisters of Oxbridge and the cafes of Hampstead; the inns of court and the teaching hospitals. London became a laboratory of ideas.

There have been more sinister émigrés, too, such as Robert Maxwell. Some of those who settled here remained implacable enemies of capitalism. After 60 years of life in Britain, Eric

Hobsbawm was yesterday still asking 'Was Marx right after all?' in the *Guardian*. But Marx and Engels themselves were exiles here, and so that tradition, too, is now hallowed by age. Without the Middle Europeans, the rest of the British Left might as well emigrate.

• *Daily Telegraph*, 21.10.98

★ ☆ ★

The English way with ideas is not to kill them but to let them die of neglect.

• Jeremy Paxman, *Observer*, 27.12.99

★ ☆ ★

Few of us have experienced a butler and even fewer have had one. Today, the term has become debased and is inaccurately applied, for instance, to P G Wodehouse's Jeeves, who was not a butler but a gentleman's gentleman.

In his heyday he was the chief manservant in households which were not grand enough to have either a steward or chamberlain. He was a person set apart, being above the rest of the servants and just below the family. He was always addressed by his surname and by inferior staff as 'Mr'. In the Victorian age his chief task was to look after the wine cellar and take care of the household accounts. He ironed the newspapers in the morning and polished the silver in the pantry.

Answering the front door was generally the task of a footman, but the butler would announce visitors as they entered the drawing-room – and he saw to it that those designated as 'persons' were firmly kept in the hall. He would also announce that dinner was served. Monosyllabic discretion was seen to be an essential virtue, plus celibacy, for to marry was viewed as a betrayal.

Today, we live in an age of hired butlers. Through the years I've arrived at endless fashionable dinner parties in London to find the same impervious face greeting me. Those in the country who can no longer afford a manservant do not hesitate to persuade a suitable villager to don the kit for a grand evening. Sometimes the result can be akin to amateur theatricals.

Would I like a butler manservant myself? No, it wouldn't suit me, and dim memories cross my mind of the fate of Dirk Bogarde in the film *The Servant*. I don't mind opening the door and I'm perfectly happy serving myself at table.

Years ago it was explained to me how the great Victorians achieved so much. The answer was a simple one: all their chores were done by someone else. I know it is a reactionary view, yet there is a lot to be said for it. But a century ago I'd have been the butler.

• Roy Strong, *Sunday Telegraph*, 3.1.99

★ ☆ ★

Early 1950s Britain was a land devoid of what we now call lifestyle. Almost everyone, young or old, wore the same drab garments and inhabited the same shabby homes. 'Housewives' in turbans and tight-waisted coats stood in queues to buy horsemeat and even whale meat. Sweets were rationed until 1953; a Mars Bar cost four old pennies and 'one point' from your ration book.

Food was universally disgusting: greyish meat, watery cabbage, slobbery milk puddings, wrinkled yellow broad beans with thick black stripes. My father, a nostalgic before his time, would speak wistfully of the unrationed plenty 'before the war' – the butter, the cheese, the huge Victoria plums. Ham was a huge delicacy, as were celery and radishes until the 1960s import boom. Fruit was so scarce that I still can't get enough of it.

Amazingly, there was no resentment that we lived under greater hardship than nations that had lost the war. There was unassailable trust in the wisdom of those who governed us; a belief that, despite the enduring bomb sites and shortages and restrictions, life really was getting better every minute. You can hear that spirit in the commentaries of cinema newsreels that presented Britain as a land of progress and social cooperation. Another hydro-electric plant opened? Another coup for British exporters? Another victory for sensible British statesmanship? I remember how even the first H-bomb explosions were presented as a triumph of dedication and teamwork.

When the 1960s began I was 17, a dejected, graceless, ignorant youth with no expectations whatever. Some time around 1961 I found myself confronted by a supper table spread with everything I believed had vanished from the earth – multicoloured salads, heaped bowls of fruit, slices of ham rolled around asparagus. 'Is everyone hungry?' my hostess asked. I remember thinking: 'This isn't the kind of food you eat when you're hungry.'

It got better even than that. It got better than the disconsolate 1950s boy ever dreamt. I discovered that failure hadn't been bred into me in the womb. I discovered that, if I really wanted to, I could do anything. Carnaby Street fashion gave me my longed-for Wild West rig of black leather, corduroy and high-heeled boots. In the evenings, I was a Ruritanian hussar. I met the Beatles, the Rolling Stones, Mary Quant, David Bailey, Harold Wilson, Elizabeth Taylor and Richard Burton. I even met Diana Dors. I sat with her by her swimming pool and watched her huge, bee-stung lips singing all the tracks from Sgt Pepper's Lonely Hearts Club Band.

Yes, if you were young – if you were me – they were great. The year 1969 was the most lingering end of any decade I can remember, packing in a symphony of last hurrahs from Woodstock and the Stones in the Park to the Beatles' Abbey

Road. The 1960s rescued me from my childhood and gave me another childhood that, perhaps, still hasn't ended. They gave me what I had never dared aspire to – happiness. The 1950s gave me nothing but a splinter of ice near my heart. I feel it whenever I see a copy of John Bull magazine, or a blue and white-ringed mug, or the twin grinning mouths of the Utility mark.

• Philip Norman, *The Sunday Times*, 21.3.99

★ ☆ ★

Anyone who has ever been to an English public school will feel comparatively at home in a prison. It is the people brought up in the gay intimacy of the slums who find prison so soul-destroying.

• Evelyn Waugh

★ ☆ ★

In France it is rude to let a conversation drop; in England it is rash to keep it up. No one in England will blame you for silence. Be modest. If you are a world tennis champion say 'Yes, I don't play too badly.' If you have crossed the Atlantic alone in a small boat, say, 'I do a little sailing.'

A golden rule is: never ask questions. For six months during World War One I lived in the same tent and shared a bath-tub with an Englishman. He never asked me if I was married, what I did in peace time or what were the books I was reading under his nose. If you insist on making confidence, they will be listened to with polite indifference.

• Andre Maurois

★ ☆ ★

In England it is bad manners to be clever, to assert something confidently. It may be your personal view that two and two makes four, but you must not state it in a self-assured way because this is a democratic country and others may be of a different opinion.

• George Mikes

★ ☆ ★

The Anglo-Saxon conscience doesn't prevent the Anglo-Saxon from sinning. It merely prevents him from enjoying it.

• George Bernard Shaw

★ ☆ ★

The English sent all their bores abroad and acquired the Empire as punishment.

• Anon

★ ☆ ★

The American novelist Tom Wolfe once said that there are restaurants in New York where if an upper-class Englishman picks up the bill, the whole table rises up and applauds.

• Jenny McCartney, *Sunday Telegraph*, 9.4.00

★ ☆ ★

Sir – Anne Applebaum reports elegantly on the lack of official emotion following her taking on our nationality, with the perceptive suggestion that only a fundamentally stable country would offer such indifference. This sounded familiar to me. In Brussels in 1945 British and Dominion prisoners returning from the Oflags and Stalags were sorted out. On arrival we met notices and banners: 'Canada welcomes you back'; 'Well done,

New Zealanders'; 'Australia is proud of you'. The British notice read: 'You are reminded that you are still under military discipline'.

• Tom Massey Lynch, letter to the *Spectator*, 13.5.00

★ ☆ ★

In Somerset people have started to throw dog biscuits into a stream in a bid to attract holidaymakers. According to the English Tourist Board's very glossy monthly newspaper, a body called the Research Into Lost Knowledge Organisation this year revived as a tourist attraction the old custom of 'Feeding the Great Hound of Langport'.

There is, apparently, a huge dog shape on the landscape near Glastonbury and the yokels there too have been persuaded to throw dog biscuits (in this case the modern equivalent of Easter cakes) from Barrow Mump into the stream forming the dog's mouth while they incant wishes for a good harvest.

Now that I rely on tourism for part of my livelihood I am fully aware of the benefits of the upsurge in the holiday trade. It has brought us jobs and foreign exchange and given a strong impetus to restore and preserve our towns, countryside and historic sights. Indeed recent reports suggest that tourism may be the country's number one industry by the end of the century.

Nonetheless I cannot help feeling a twinge of unease at the way our national customs, habits and eccentricities are increasingly being staged to create 'tourist attractions'. Like South Sea islanders in their grass skirts and garlands of flowers, we dance attendance attired in absurd fancy dress as we revive long forgotten (and probably best forgotten) customs.

Until recently we were casual to the point of indifference about our heritage. Beefeaters at the Tower, sentries in their bearskins at the Royal palaces were there for reasons of tradition and if they happened to attract tourists that was an incidental benefit. Now we are going to the other extreme.

There is a trend towards doing things, not because they are worth doing in themselves, but because they make a sight for camera-slinging tourists. What will be next? Will we see the owners of stately homes donning ermine and coronets to greet the sightseers? What about Hansom cabs outside Baker Street station? Perhaps it would be possible to recreate in a corner of Docklands a good old-fashioned pea-souper fog for all those Americans – and Russians – in search of the London of Charles Dickens?

• Evelyn Cox, *Daily Telegraph*, 4.9.85

14 Living In The Dark

films

Film is drama at its most impatient.

- Nicholas Hytner, Film and Stage Director (*Miss Saigon, The Madness of King George*)

★ ☆ ★

In François Dupeyron's latest film, *C'est Quoi la Vie?* (What's Life?), a French farmer contemplates suicide. In Cedric Kahn's *L'Ennui* (Boredom), a depressed teacher embarks on a doomed affair. In Marion Vernoux's *Rien à Faire* (Nothing to Do), a pair of sacked workers seek solace in the dole queue.

However, all these recent French films are models of cheerfulness compared to the latest product of the Parisian school dubbed cinematic miserablism.

In *Resources Humaines* (Human Resources), Laurent Cantet breaks new ground in paralysing pessimism. His unwatchable film about evil bosses and militant workers in a factory negotiating new labour contracts – with amateur actors in all but one of the principal roles – may prove to be a turning point in the French government's attempts to force-feed elitist culture to the European masses.

The sad truth about Cantet's film is that few people outside France – and not that many inside – are likely to be interested in a gruelling dramatised account of union negotiations over reducing the working week to 35 hours. In *Resources Humaines* there is no romance and few jokes and nobody takes off their clothes.

• Tony Allen-Mills, *Sunday Times*, 23.1.00

★ ☆ ★

He cannot get the bums on seats. Lord Puttnam of Queen's Gate, the film producer, had an awkward time addressing the Tiverton Labour Society. 'There was only one person in the audience but he applauded wildly and made up for the lack of numbers. When I finished my talk I said, "There isn't much point in having a question and answer session, so I think I'll pack up and catch my train." ' His listener registered grave disappointment and said he would greatly appreciate his staying. 'When I asked him why my presence was so important, he replied, "I'm the next speaker." '

★ ☆ ★

The Russian picture, *Hands*, is one of the most disturbing films you will ever see – if, that is, you want to see it. Its heroes are Dostoevsky's Insulted And Injured: a man who moves around in a broken bath-tub, a woman who has lain on the ground for 40 years, a rag collector building a pile of rubbish to reach the sky, a dumb boy who has escaped from an asylum to live in a hovel in the ground, an old hunchback who keeps the head of her executioner in a wooden box, a blind beggar family who work the streets of Kishinev. Collectively, they make for one of the most miserable nights out at the cinema you're likely to get.

• Isobel Montgomery, *Guardian*, 28.8.98

★ ☆ ★

Treasured movie lines often tread that perilous line between good and bad. In *I Was A Teenage Frankenstein*, Professor

Frankenstein rebukes his new creation with the words: 'I know you've got a civil tongue in your head because I sewed it there myself.'

It is the worst lines that retain their baroque grandeur – such as 'A brass unicorn has been catapulted across a London street and impaled an eminent surgeon. Words fail me!' (spoken in *The Abominable Doctor Phibes*, 1971).

Cinema's equivalent of the Victoria Cross should go to those actors who have grappled with such lines. Heaven knows what the distinguished Italian actor Giancarlo Giannini thought when he went to Hollywood to co-star in the Keanu Reeves vehicle *A Walk In The Clouds* and got saddled with the line: 'Don't think because I speak with an accent that I think with an accent!'

And no matter how long Stephen Dorff's career may last, he will never have to show more courage than he did in uttering this impassioned accusation in the thriller *Innocent Lies*: 'Your mother was strangled with the catgut from your racket!'

Paradoxically, good lines in screenplays – because they sound natural – are soon forgotten. The lines that stick in the mind are the terrible ones. Was there ever a line more mawkish or self-satisfied than Ryan O'Neal's in *Love Story*: 'She loved Mozart and Bach, the Beatles, and me.'?

Horror fans would be hard put to utter a good line from any of their favourite movies, but they can usually be relied upon to remember exclamations like 'An intellectual carrot – the mind boggles!' (from *The Thing*), or from *Night of the Lepus*: 'There's a herd of killer rabbits heading this way!'

In historical dramas, the most memorable lines tend to be the most unauthentic ones. Cleopatra is remembered not only for epic set-pieces such as the entry of Elizabeth Taylor into Rome, but also for the inadequate verbal response to this marvel: 'Nothing like this has come to Rome since Romulus and Remus!'

Screenplays for medieval movies have a particularly ignoble history, with bathetic lines such as Virginia Mayo's to George

Sanders in *King Richard and the Crusaders*: 'War! War! That's all you think of, Dick Plantagenet! You burner! You pillager!' And there's Loretta Young's instruction to King Richard in *The Crusades*: 'You've just gotta save Christianity, Richard! You gotta!'

The really memorable lines are those which try to be romantic but fail miserably. I, for one, was never able to take Alain Delon seriously after seeing him murmur a series of disastrous chat-up lines to Marianne Faithfull in *Girl on a Motorcycle* (1968), including, 'Your toes are like tombstones.'

Luciano Pavarotti had a corker in *Yes, Giorgio* (1982) when he crooned: 'You are a thirsty plant, Pamela. Giorgio can water you.'

• Christopher Tookey, *Daily Mail*, 7.10.99

★ ☆ ★

When James Coburn won an Oscar on Sunday as Best Supporting Actor, the orchestra had to start playing to get him to finish his acceptance speech. The record-holder for the longest acceptance speech remains Greer Garson, who spoke for five-and-a-half minutes in 1943 after winning for *Mrs Miniver*. And Laurence Olivier didn't do badly in 1979 when, accepting a lifetime achievement award, he embarked on a baroque peroration that ended with the words: 'From the top of this moment, in the solace, in the kindly emotion that is charging my soul and heart at this moment, I thank you for this great gift which lends me such a very splendid part in this, your glorious occasion.'

Drawing on the experience of the Oscars, the new International Academy of Digital Arts and Sciences has imposed a drastic new rule for its Webby Awards for the best Web sites in cyberspace: no acceptance speech may exceed five words. At last Thursday's awards ceremony in San Francisco, some winners ran to seven or even eight words, but generally the rule was obeyed. 'Thank you. We deserve it,' went one speech. 'Ugly commercial sons of bitches,' went another.

• Alexander Chancellor, *Daily Telegraph*, 23.3.99

★ ☆ ★

Contrary to worldwide opinion, not all of Washington has been consumed this year by speculation about who did what to whom in the corridor outside the Oval Office. This month, virtually unnoticed by the newspapers, the US Congress took a step that radically affects its entire entertainment industry. Hollywood is jubilant; it will bring the film studios billions of dollars in extra revenue. So, too, is the American music business, which will also profit vastly.

Why? Because Congress has quietly approved a Bill to extend the American copyright term – already a generous 75 years for films – by a further 20 years. Incredible but true. It will now be nearly a century from its release date before an old movie enters the 'public domain' in America.

There are two ways of looking at this. You may feel that Hollywood has made such a wonderful contribution to civilisation that it deserves every extra dollar it can get. Or you can take the view that this whole damn copyright business has got completely out of hand.

Consider the historical perspective. Shakespeare, Mozart, Beethoven, Leonardo da Vinci and J S Bach would have been bemused by the whole notion of owning 'rights' to the expression of an idea. A baker would not dream of stipulating how his customers sliced his bread after they bought it, and neither would any composer, writer or artist until modern times have expected 'rights' over a work of art after its delivery to the person who commissioned it.

Indeed, if an image or a tune was copied, it was regarded more as a compliment than a rip-off. Mozart copied from, and vastly improved upon, Salieri. Shakespeare cribbed nearly all of his plots. Handel, as a contemporary noted, habitually 'took other men's pebbles and polished them into diamonds'. It was a free-for-all, but everybody knew the score – and it saved a hell of a lot of legal fees.

What annoys me is that, when governments legislate on entertainment matters, they get plenty of heavy 'advice' from showbiz interests, but nobody is there to speak up for the poor bloody consumers. Why should a big corporation have the exclusive right to exploit the work of creative geniuses from almost a century earlier? After we have taken care of an author's immediate heirs, art or music or literature or film should be seen as a common cultural heritage, freely available to all.

• Richard Morrison, *The Times*, 23.10.98

★ ☆ ★

Louis B Mayer, when he was head of the film studio, MGM, was asked how he could justify being paid much more than the President of the United States, replied, 'Well, look at my responsibilities.'

★ ☆ ★

At a London dinner party a playwright, one of the guests, asked Charlie Chaplin about a film script showing a fat lady slipping on a banana peel. What was the best way to get a laugh out of that cliché situation? Was the best way first to show the banana peel, then cut to the fat lady approaching and then she slips on it, or is it more effective to show the fat lady first and then the banana peel and then she slips. 'Neither,' said Chaplin. 'You show the fat lady approaching, then you cut to the banana peel, then you show the fat lady and the banana peel together.

Then you show the fat lady stepping over the banana peel, and disappearing down a manhole.'

• Overheard by Milton Shulman

★ ☆ ★

At a French airport, Sir Alfred Hitchcock, the master of suspense thrillers, was held up by a French immigration official who was suspicious about Hitchcock's passport which listed his occupation simply as 'Producer'. 'What do you produce?' asked the official. 'Gooseflesh,' was Hitchcock's reply.

• *Faber Book of Anecdotes*, edited by Clifton Fadiman

Sir Alfred Hitchcock

15 Better Than Sex

food and wine

After a most convivial dinner with very dear friends – beef on the bone followed by chocolate sponge on the bone, then a little bone on the bone to suck with coffee – our host invited each of us to pick the single word that, in our opinion, might best sum up the 20th century. A thoughtful hush descended upon the assembled company, a hush broken only by the distinctive tick-tock of the grandfather clock (no digital nonsense in *that* household, if you please, Monsieur Jospin!). It was my own good self who broke the silence. 'The word is *tiresome*,' I piped up. 'We can all agree that it has been an immensely *tiresome* century.'

My choice was greeted with a murmur of approval. But what, asked our host – a regular panellist on the Home Service's *Round Britain Quiz* – what did we feel to be the single most tiresome aspect of this most tiresome of centuries? Suggestions came in thick and fast – the television, the 'Y-front', air travel, the portable toothbrush, 'jogging', public transport, the gramaphone. But, once again, it was I who put my finger on it. 'Chewing-gum!' I exclaimed, pronouncing it in my humorous 'cockney' voice ('choowin' garm'). We all agreed that Mr Wrigley (dread name!) had much to answer for, though his answer would doubtless be inaudible, his mouth being chock-a-block with his stringy comestible.

• Wallace Arnold, *Spectator* 1.1.00

* ☆ *

It Takes All Sorts

When I left my wife, Drusilla Beyfus, in labour in hospital for our first child, her final words to me as I left were: 'Remember! Champagne, jewellery, roses and foie gras!'

• Milton Shulman

★ ☆ ★

My daughter, Alexandra, at the age of five was playing with her dolls and planning a party for them. Talking to one doll she was overheard saying: 'It's not going to be a smart party – just whisky, wine and milk.'

• Milton Shulman

★ ☆ ★

Funny buggers, chefs. The first time I realized quite how weirdly Twilight Zone they were was when I went to interview a chef at the Garrick Club. This was years before I did this as a job, and I could rarely afford to eat in restaurants. My experience of chefs was limited to watching a bloke in Pizza Express and a striped T-shirt trying to stick dough to the ceiling.

I can't even remember why I was interviewing the chef at the Garrick (not one of the present incumbents, I hasten to add). He looked like he'd been pickled in brine, then larded with back fat. He sat on a small stool, hunched over a slimy bucket of roots, in a subterranean kitchen that must have been designed by Jules Verne and which got a light surface-wiping every leap year.

I asked him something original like 'What do you do, then?' He looked left and right, grabbed my lapel and, with a desperate whisper of tartare breath, said: 'This is off the record. This mustn't leave these four walls. Understand?' He tapped the handle of his 12 in. Sabatier. 'I have a secret role. Up there.' He pointed his blade to the pus-yellow stalactite ceiling. 'Up there, the most powerful people in Britain meet in secret. Judges, generals, magnates, aristocrats. And they organise the world.

They arrange things. Everything. You think you live in a democracy.' He smiled pityingly and prodded the ceiling again for emphasis. 'You mean the Garrick is really a front for a secret organisation, like Smersh?' 'That's fiction. That's kids' stuff. Up there, they're fomenting revolution and the rest of you don't even notice. This is the engine room. My steak and kidney is at the heart of it.'

Cross my heart, I'm not making this up. It may not be the word for word, but this boned-and-rolled, deep-fried dingbat really thought he was part of a vast Establishment conspiracy that ruled the universe. And he never went upstairs. He wasn't allowed upstairs. To my certain knowledge, upstairs there was a snoozing recorder of the Family Division, a gay farce impresario, Keith Waterhouse and a man who'd had a good war, all discussing Celia Johnson's breasts.

'How long have you worked here,' I asked, backing towards the door. 'Forty years.' 'Forty years peeling potatoes?' 'This isn't peeling potatoes. This is passing the ammunition.' It was only much later, when I became professionally involved, that I realized this bloke was actually quite understated, quite balanced for a chef. Heavens, some of them have whites with sleeves that tie up at the back.

A A Gill, Style supplement, *Sunday Times*, 2.1.00

★ ☆ ★

As the biting winds of autumn sweep across the land, Mayte Garcia – the wife of the Artist, formerly known as Squiggle and Prince – is on hand to provide us all with a delicious, warming recipe for those long dark evenings. It is for a dish called 'Love Soup'.

This recipe – details of which follow below – was inspired by some very non-Delia Smith sentiments that Mayte and the former Squiggle appear to share. 'We are vegetarian for love reasons,' Mayte explains, 'for our love of animals. It isn't really much of an effort for us to give up eating meat and fish. As a child, I already liked pasta better than meat. And Prince too. I cook at home. I love cooking. And I make this delicious soup, his favourite, which he baptised "Love Soup".'

So here is the recipe for those who might wish to try it at home. 'You make it with all kinds of vegetables, fried tomatoes, garlic and onions,' says Mayte. After that, she adds, 'you let it simmer for a while, then you add some rice. And a large pinch of love, of course.' Of course. Elizabeth David would surely have approved.

• Peterborough, *The Daily Telegraph*, 13.10.98

★ ☆ ★

'If something terrible happens,' Charles Bukowski wrote in *Women*, 'you drink to forget it; if something good happens you drink to celebrate...and if nothing happens, you drink to make something happen.'

• Declan O'Neill, *Independent*, 11.11.98, reviewing *Locked in the Arms of a Crazy Life* by Howard Sounes

★ ☆ ★

Not having watched a TV cookery programme since the days of Fanny Cradock, I was amazed to learn from Michel Roux that there are now 45 food programmes a week. That's a lot of sun-dried tomatoes.

The celebrity chef complains of an excess of celebrity chefs, saying that cooking has been turned into a game show, and adding: 'When you go to a restaurant, you go to eat. You do not want a chef going round the tables, glass in hand, spilling wine, telling a joke and saying the occasional rude word.'

Hear hear to that. Whenever I see the chef poncing around a restaurant and sitting down uninvited with some famous diner, I wonder who's doing the cooking, just as I wonder who's driving the aeroplane when the captain comes down the aisle to chat up the passengers.

I expect they imagine that by pausing at a table to graciously accept gushing praise for the lentil puree they endow the punter with a sprinkle of their own stardom. In that case they should put it on the bill along with the cover charge and the 'optional' 12 1/2 percent.

I blame the food critics. Before restaurants started to be reviewed like theatrical first nights, chefs were content to slave over a hot stove. Now every chef wants his name in lights.

• Keith Waterhouse, *Daily Mail*, 5.10.98

★ ☆ ★

Andrew Lloyd Webber was suspicious that all was not well with the '82s. He thought some of them decidedly thin and dodgy. The fact that he owns several hundred thousand pounds' worth of the stuff didn't mean he was blind to its shortcomings. He was, I suspect, a bit miffed that Auberon Waugh had written a piece in the *Spectator* on 26 September, pouring scorn on the 1982 vintage – The Château Léoville-Les Cases, according to Waugh, was 'a thin, short, defeatist little wine, with nothing more to come out of it.'

'Defeatist', eh? Could we match Mr Waugh's elegant scorn? Could I, more to the point, find anything to say on the matter? I, whose appreciation of wine stops at Sainsbury's Nuits St Georges for big occasions, and Châteauneuf-du-Pape for Sunday lunch?

The tasting began. We shuffled round the table like monks around a cloister. The Montrose was, I noted, 'plummy on the nose, flat as a flounder on the palate.' The La Lagune smelt OK, but was (can I believe I wrote this?) 'short as a Finnish night.' 'No good, no good,' said Lloyd Webber. 'It's just not going anywhere.' The Ducru-Beaucaillou had sweet undernotes (sweet claret?), but everyone noddingly agreed that it would 'improve'. The Lynch Bages was soft and yummy and smelt of hay, while the Cos d'Estournel was 'disastrously bitter and medicinal.' One guest gushed, 'I've just tried the Pichon Lalande, and it's a very *pretty* little girl.'

And then I tasted the Château Latour, and began to tingle from head to foot. It lay on my tongue like a dream, spread itself languorously to the corners of my mouth, and took off in a million directions at once.

'Bloody hell,' was all I could say. The wine merchant looked up. 'Incredibly long finish,' he observed. 'That's the secret. That's where the money is.'

And I only realized that it was the best wine in the world because, for the first time, all the adjectives deserted me.

• Craig Brown, on claret-tasting *chez* the Lloyd Webbers, *Independent*, 12.10.98

★ ☆ ★

The joy of chicken is rarely celebrated in song, though I used to enjoy playing an old 78 rpm record called 'Pickin' a Chicken', in which the lady singer jauntily tried to persuade her suitor to go to a carnival and start pickin' a chicken with her. Who knows? Perhaps this was a metaphor for something more saucy, but if so it was lost on me then, and remains lost on me now.

But it's hard to find many other hymns of praise to the glory of chicken. Mahler wrote no *Chicken Symphony*. Wagner never wrote *The Ride of the Poultry*. Even Andrew Lloyd Webber went for the easy cat option rather than trying to break new ground with chickens. In fact, the only other chicken in the history of music was a 1969 album called *Hundred Ton Chicken* by the relatively obscure heavy rock group Chicken Shack.

Food critics, too, tend to shy away from chicken. I suspect this is because they feel snooty towards anything too popular. Toast is hardly ever mentioned by food critics, for instance, yet it's the favourite dish of everyone I know. I can't think of any normal person who doesn't love chicken. Even some vegetarians seem to have elected it an honorary vegetable.

• Craig Brown, *Sunday Telegraph*, 13.12.98

★ ☆ ★

There is nothing which has yet been contrived by man, by which so much happiness is produced as by a good tavern or inn.

• Samuel Johnson

★ ☆ ★

What I most don't like about the theatre bar is how nothing at all has changed around it and how impossible it still is to get a pre-performance drink.

Never enough staff. Night after night the pair behind the bar go into a blind panic, as though a thirsting theatre crowd is a brand new experience for them. This has been going on since 1563. Had the management known it was going to be busy this particular evening, they would have hired extra help. But how could they have known? It's only David Garrick playing opposite Sarah Bernhardt in Strindberg's Miss Julie with music by Stephen Sondheim.

There are two schools of thought on how to get a drink in a theatre. Some say you take up a position at the bar and stay there. Others favour the opportunistic dart. You spy an opening, you see the barman edging towards it, and you pounce. If it's your lucky night the barman takes your order to the exasperation of everyone who hasn't moved a millimetre since the night before. If luck's against you the barman discovers your ploy, remembers something he'd forgotten, and pirouettes back to that section of the bar where you were previously standing, clearing it in ten seconds.

A third school of thought, of which I am Emeritus Professor, Vice-Chancellor and Governing Body, maintains there is always something to be gained by running from one end of the bar to the other, neither joining any line nor leaping into any vacant space, but simply getting hot under the collar and voicing strenuous objections.

I thought I'd hit the jackpot the other night, finding one solitary teetotaller in front of me, paying, as it appeared, for a single shandy; but then came his interval order – two dozen white wines, half of them dry, half of them sweet; eight glasses of champagne, half of them *brut*, half of them *extra-brut*... When the barman had finally totted him up and got around to asking what he could do for me, I was so overwrought I told him 'In your dreams, sunshine!' and stormed off drinkless. Fine by way of relieving my feelings, but less satisfactory for the company I was keeping, who without ado approached the bar and grabbed herself a stiff gin.

• Howard Jacobson, Weekend Review, *Independent*, 25.9.99

★ ☆ ★

Old friends, old wine and old books are said to be the mainstay of a stable life. According to Norris McWhirter's *Book of Millennium Records*, archaeologists excavating a site in Iran have found a stoppered pottery jar that dates from *c.*4000 BC. It contained wine. Enquiring minds wonder whether it was a good year.

• Pandora, *Independent*, 29.7.99

★ ☆ ★

You will see that we have given into local pressure and are supplying a special menu of prawn cocktails, steak, chips, peas and tomatoes. On the day that this outsells the other menu, I will shoot myself.

• Notice by a Welsh restaurateur

★ ☆ ★

When the insects take over the world, we hope they'll remember we took them along to all our picnics.

• Anon

★ ☆ ★

Three dishes are the minimum for a proper Chinese meal. They used to serve three even in Chinese police stations.

• Kenneth Lo, restaurateur

16 More About Goldberg

Jewish jokes

Goldberg went into a cheap restaurant feeling depressed. When the waiter asked him what he wanted he said: 'A couple of soft-boiled eggs and a few kind words.' Five minutes later the eggs arrived and Goldberg sighed, 'Alright, now I got the eggs. How about the few kind words.' The waiter leaned over and whispered in Goldberg's ear, 'Don't eat those eggs.'

⋆ ☆ ⋆

Cohen visiting his old friend Goldberg said, 'Goldberg, at our age when we are alone, the children far away, it is important to have an interesting hobby.'

'I have a hobby,' said Goldberg.

'Ah! What is it?'

'Bees. I keep bees.'

Cohen looked out of the window. 'So where is the hive?'

'I don't use a hive. I keep them in my bedroom.'

'In your bedroom! Don't the bees sting you?'

'How can they sting me? I keep them in the cupboard.'

'But when you open the cupboard door, the bees could fly out.'

'They can't. I keep them in a box.'

'Inside a box? You punched holes in the box?'

'Why should I punch holes in the box?' asked Goldberg.

'For air. Oxygen. If they don't get air, the bees will die,' said Cohen.

'So?'

'So! What's the matter with you, Goldberg? Don't you care if all your bees die?'

Goldberg shrugged his shoulders. 'It's only a hobby.'

* ☆ *

Goldberg visiting a cemetery in Paris saw a magnificent, marble mausoleum on which was inscribed the one word ROTHSCHILD. 'Ai! Ai! Ai!' exclaimed Goldberg, rolling his head from side to side. 'Now that's what I call living.'

* ☆ *

Jews are great worriers. Two elderly Jews sat in silence on a park bench for hours lost in thought. Finally one of them sighed deeply and uttered a long and languid 'Oy!' The other replied, 'You're telling me!'

* ☆ *

Goldberg is keen to join Cohen's expensive golf club but Cohen warns him that the club is very exclusive and demanding about its conventions. For example, Goldberg must get himself a more acceptable car like a Rolls Royce or a Mercedes instead of his rather battered Cortina. A few days later Goldberg phones Cohen to tell him that he has followed his advice and purchased a handsome Silver Shadow Rolls. Cohen interjects, 'Are you calling me from a public call-box? Can that be true?' Goldberg shamefacedly admits he is in a call-box whereupon Cohen tells him that everyone in the club has a phone in his car and he should have one installed if he wants to become a member. A few days later, travelling to the club to meet the committee that will interview him about his membership, Goldberg's Rolls Royce stops at a red traffic light and Goldberg notices that Cohen's car is right behind him. He tells his chauffeur to phone Cohen's car so that he can talk to him. 'Hello, Cohen,' says Goldberg. 'You see that car in front of you? Well that's mine. And I'm meeting the committee about my membership. And as you can hear, I've listened to your instructions and I have the right car with a telephone installed in it.' To which Cohen replies, 'And you got me out of my bath just to tell me that!'

★ ☆ ★

Goldberg having ordered a pair of trousers from his tailor, Mr Cohen, was constantly told by his tailor that the trousers were not yet ready. He had numerous excuses for the delay. He was ill, his wife was ill, the material was difficult to get. Exasperated when told again the trousers were not ready, Goldberg said: 'Look, Cohen, it's already taken you six weeks and you still haven't got my pants ready.'

'So?' said the tailor.

'So, you ask! Six weeks for a pair of pants! Goodness, it took God only six days to create the Universe.'

'So,' shrugged the tailor. 'Just look at it.'

★ ☆ ★

Every Jewish mother wants her son to get married – until she finds there is a girl involved.

- Jackie Mason joke after comedienne Roseanne Barr advertised for three Jewish men to marry her three daughters. Quoted in *Mail on Sunday* 22.11.98

★ ☆ ★

After months of negotiation, a Jewish scholar from Odessa was granted permission to visit Moscow. He boarded the train and found an empty seat. At the next stop a young man got on and sat next to him. The scholar looked at the young man and thought:

This fellow doesn't look like a peasant, and if he isn't a peasant, he probably comes from this district. If he comes from this district, he must be Jewish because this is, after all, a Jewish district. On the other hand, if he is a Jew, where could he be going? I'm the only one in our district who has permission to travel to Moscow.

Wait – just outside Moscow there is a little village called Samvet, and you don't need special permission to go there. But why would he be going to Samvet? He's probably going to visit somebody there, but how many Jewish families are there in Samvet? Only two – the Bernsteins and the Steinbergs. The Bernsteins are a terrible family, so he must be visiting the Steinbergs. But why is he going?

The Steinbergs have only girls, so maybe he's their son-in-law. But if he is, then which daughter did he marry? Sarah married that nice lawyer from Budapest and Esther married a businessman from Zhadomir, so it must be Sarah's husband. Which means that his name is Alexander Cohen, if I'm not mistaken. But if he comes from Budapest, with all the anti-Semitism they have there, he must have changed his name. What's the Hungarian equivalent of Cohen? Kovacs. But if he changed his name, he must have some special status. What could it be? A doctorate from the university.

At this point the scholar turned to the young man and said, 'How do you do, Dr Kovacs?'

'Very well, thank you, sir,' answered the startled passenger. 'But how is it that you know my name?'

'Oh,' replied the scholar, 'it was obvious.'

• *Big Book of Jewish Humour*, ed. William Novak & Moshie Waldoks

★ ☆ ★

Goldberg visits a kosher Chinese restaurant in Soho, and to his great surprise, the Chinese waiter addresses him in Yiddish.

On the way out, as he is paying the bill, he says to the proprietor, 'You run a nice restaurant. And a Chinese waiter who speaks Yiddish – what a wonderful gimmick that is.'

'Not so loud,' says the proprietor. 'He thinks we're teaching him English.'

* ☆ *

Goldberg walks into a jewellery shop to buy his wife a present. 'How much is this?' he asks the clerk, pointing to a sterling silver crucifix.

'That's £400, sir,' replies the clerk.

'Nice,' says Goldberg. 'And without the acrobat?'

* ☆ *

I am of a Semitic background – I *assume* I'm Jewish. A lot of Jews who think they're Jewish are not – they're switched babies.

Now, a Jew, in the dictionary, is one who is descended from the ancient tribe of Judea, or one who is regarded as descended from that tribe. That's what it says in the dictionary; but you and I know what a Jew is – *One Who Killed Our Lord*. I don't know if we got much press on that in Illinois – we did this about two thousand years ago – two thousand years of Polack kids whacking the shit out of us coming home from school. Why do you keep breaking our balls for this crime?

'Why, Jew, because you skirt the issue. You blame it on Roman soldiers.'

All right. I'll clear the air once and for all, and confess. Yes, we did it. I did it, my family. I found a note in my basement. It said:

'We killed him.

'signed,

'Morty.'

It Takes All Sorts

And a lot of people say to me, 'Why did you kill Christ?'

'I dunno… It was one of those parties – got out of hand, you know.'

We killed him because he didn't want to become a doctor, that's why we killed him.

• Lenny Bruce, quoted in *Big Book of Jewish Humour*, ed. William Novak & Moshie Waldoks

★ ☆ ★

Goldberg for the first time in his life went into a non-kosher delicatessen and bought some tomatoes. With elaborate insouciance he asked for the first time in his life, 'By the way, how much costs the bacon?' Came a terrible flash of lightening and a clap of thunder. Goldberg looked up at the heavens and protested, 'I was only asking.'

★ ☆ ★

When Mrs Goldberg was told that her son had bought a yacht and was therefore now a sea captain, she said, 'To you he may be a captain and to me he may be a captain, but to a captain is he a captain?'

★ ☆ ★

Goldberg answered the door and a stranger announced himself as Jack the Ripper. 'Bella!' called out Goldberg. 'It's for you.'

17 In The Long Run, You're Dead

health, medicine and doctors

In his novel *Catch 22*, Joseph Heller has a character who collected lists of fatal diseases and arranged them in alphabetical order so he could put his finger without delay on anybody he wanted to worry about.

★ ☆ ★

When Elizabeth I suffered from a severe toothache, she howled so much night and day that the Palace could get no sleep. Finally one of the courtiers assured her that getting a tooth pulled was not a painful experience. To prove his point he had the local dental extractor pull out two of his healthy teeth and smilingly showed his mouth to the Queen. Thus re-assured, the Queen undertook the operation and the Palace got some sleep.

★ ☆ ★

As reassuring as a dentist with an instruction manual.

★ ☆ ★

Having burnt my thumb, I tried to get an appointment with a busy dermatologist and was told by his secretary that the earliest time he could see me was in six weeks. Having burnt my thumb on a hot towel rail, I urged the secretary to tell the doctor that I was in great pain and would appreciate an earlier appointment. She spoke to the doctor and returned saying that in view of my condition he would see me in 48 hours.

When I arrived he bustled in crying 'Where's this Burma thumb?'

'I haven't got a Burma thumb,' I said, puzzled by his question.

'Nurse,' he said, turning to his assistant, 'didn't you say he had a Burma thumb? I thought it was some form of tropical skin disease he'd contracted in the Far East.'

'No,' I said, 'I have a burnt thumb.'

'I told you it was a burnt thumb,' said the nurse.

'Oh, alright,' said the doctor, disconsolately, 'let's take a look at it.' His interest was obviously evaporating. 'I was looking forward to something exciting like a Burma thumb.'

• Milton Shulman

★ ☆ ★

I've just read a fascinating article in the new edition of the American magazine, *The Skeptical Inquirer*. It's about risk, and the bizarre and irrational way we all react to it. How is it, for example, that while we are in far more danger driving to the airport than we are flying in the plane, it's in the air that we're afraid?

The author, K C Cole, makes this point. Suppose that smoking was perfectly safe, but the manufacturers had decided that they would put a high-explosive charge in one cigarette in every 18,250 packets, a charge so strong that when lit it would immediately take your head off.

That would cause 1,600 or so fatalities in the US alone, every single day. The papers would be full of articles about smokers blown to smithereens in front of their own children. Naturally nobody at all would smoke. Yet 1,600 is roughly the number of daily deaths from smoking-related diseases in the States and the same, proportionately, here. Most people die after months of prolonged agony, beside which instantly losing your head would be positively pleasant.

• Simon Hoggart, *Guardian*, 26.9.98

★ ☆ ★

Luis Buñuel's passion for tobacco, meanwhile, equals his love of alcohol, 'It's a joy for all the senses. What lovelier sight is there than that double row of white cigarettes, lined up like soldiers on parade, wrapped in silver paper? I love to touch the pack in my pocket, open it, savour the feel of the cigarette between my fingers, the paper on my lips, the taste of tobacco on my tongue. I love to watch the flame spurt up, love to watch it come closer and closer, filling me with its warmth.'

• Review, *Independent*, 31.10.98

★ ☆ ★

A Californian laboratory technician has invented a board game in which players try to pass on infectious diseases to their rivals. At the start of Infection, conceived by Dan Sullivan, each player has five cards, representing diseases that range from anthrax to the common cold. Players die when they accumulate four of the most serious diseases.

• *Sunday Times*, 10.1.99

★ ☆ ★

I gave up smoking once again on 1 January, and am now part of the superior fraternity who can look on nicotine addicts as benighted souls, more to be pitied than scorned. But I was a little alarmed to hear about the Canadian government's new proposals for getting people off the weed. (Canada, you must remember, is at the forefront of world culture and, whatever fad they embrace today, we shall surely embrace next week. Just think – log tables, policemen with large hats, Leonard Cohen...). They have decided to go to town on smokers, but to do it with visual shock treatment. If the government's will prevails, every packet of fags sold in Canada will come festooned, across at least half its surface area, with horrible images of lungs covered in tumours, and of damaged hearts.

In a manic, what-the-hell-let's-throw-everything-at-them final flourish, they'll even insist on warning men that smoking will affect your, ahem, little fireman ('Tobacco use can make you impotent. Cigarettes may cause sexual impotence due to decreased flow to the penis') – but before you ask, no there isn't a photograph to illustrate this particular disability, only a picture of some drooping fag-ash.

I'm surprised they don't tell you your nose will fall off, your tongue will turn blue and a bear will eat you up. It's pathetic to see the state authorities coming on so vehement and nannyish, when the people they're trying to save from nicotine hell are beyond reason, and smoke precisely because it's dangerous and bad for you. As for the suggestion that cigarettes make you impotent, I suppose that would account for the pissed-off expression on Humphrey Bogart's face in all his movies, (or what you can see of it through the clouds of Craven A).

• John Walsh, *Independent*, 24.1.00

★ ☆ ★

It's 11 o'clock, I've been up since eight, I've smoked 10 cigarettes, and written 11 words, not counting these ones, or these ones. Cigarettes and writing are inseparable; fags are the fuel that drives the word, and mine don't run particularly efficiently. My vocabulary is large and flashy, a top-of-the range nicotine guzzler. I get about 20 snouts to a thousand words in the city, 15 in the country. This column is 30 fags long.

As an old lung at this smoking lark, I've learnt to measure life in terms of cigarettes. Dinner is two cigarettes per course, and three per cup of coffee. Speaking on the telephone is chain-smoking, but I'm trying to cut down and not talk for more than five at a time. Sex used to be four cigarettes, but it's now only two – I'm not as young or experimental as I was. Aimless country-walking, something I try to avoid, is measured between a two-fag stroll and a 10-gasper hike. Since I was 15, cigarettes have been my constant companions. I would no more step out of the house without my silver cigarette case than without ladies' underwear. If I had to choose between having my wallet nicked or my fags, it's no contest. You can't smoke your credit card in a rage. When on occasion I'm asked by groups of aspiring writers what they should do to get on, my advice is always, emphatically, smoke. Smoke often, and smoke with gusto. It's a little-known, indeed little-researched fact of literature and journalism that no non-smoker is worth reading. And writers who give up become crashing bores.

• A A Gill, *The Sunday Times*, 25.7.99

* ☆ *

In *The Man Who Mistook His Wife For a Hat*, Oliver Sacks records the case of Dr P, a distinguished musician who showed no sign of dementia in the ordinary sense: 'He was a man of great cultivation and charm, who talked well and fluently, with imagination and humour.' Nevertheless, Sacks noted, 'there was something a bit odd.' Although Dr P's eyesight was good, he sometimes patted the heads of fire-hydrants and parking meters, assuming them to be children; he would also speak to grand-father clocks 'and be astounded when they did not reply'.

Sacks decided that Dr P was suffering from a rare form of agnosia which prevented him from making cognitive judgments: 'A judgment is intuitive, personal, comprehensive, and concrete

– we "see" how things stand, in relation to one another and oneself. It was precisely this seeing, this relating, that Dr P lacked.'

• Francis Wheen, *Guardian*, 22.12.99

★ ☆ ★

Once, in the depths of depression, I was referred by a friend to an orthodox Freudian analyst. For 50 minutes, twice a week, I would sit in his immaculately beige office on the Upper East Side of Manhattan, blubbing hysterically, while he gazed at me in a cool, sphinxy silence. Then, I would trudge home, feeling more lonely and desperate than ever.

Eventually I stopped going. Whatever analysts do, they certainly don't offer 'solutions' for depressed young women having boyfriend problems. But I can't bring myself to dismiss the brilliance of Freud because of that. That would be like rubbishing *Das Kapital* because it hadn't given me any good tips on balancing my cheque book. If you want to be cheered up, take Prozac, read the Mars and Venus books – whatever – but don't castigate poor Sigmund. He did give us the Unconscious, after all.

• Zoe Heller, *Sunday Times*, 18.10.98

18 History Never Repeats Itself; Historians Do

history

The 20th Century never found a voice. There has been much noise but in the end no concert; much movement, unbelievable change, but in the end no map, no transfiguration. For all the agitation, we end our century far closer to what we started than did the *fin de siècle* Britain of 1899. Edwardian England was born a million miles away from the England of 1799. The 21st-Century England of Elizabeth II will still be on nodding terms with Queen Victoria.

• Matthew Parris, *The Times* 18.12.99

★ ☆ ★

That men do not learn very much from the lessons of history is the most important of all the lessons that history has to teach.

• Aldous Huxley

★ ☆ ★

Only the future is certain. The past is always changing.

• Paul Flynn MP in *Dragons Led by Poodles*

★ ☆ ★

It Takes All Sorts

Who controls the past controls the future, who controls the present controls the past.

• George Orwell, *Nineteen Eighty Four*, 1949

★ ☆ ★

April 1797 – George II ordered a party in Green Park to celebrate the end of the war of Austrian succession. Handel wrote Music for the Royal Fireworks to mark the occasion, but it was not a success. The 'Temple of Peace' was burnt down by fireworks, and three spectators were killed. And the temple's Italian architect was arrested after brawling with the king's Comptroller of Fireworks.

• *Sunday Times*, 26.12.99

★ ☆ ★

My favourite historical parallel is the famous Abraham Lincoln and John F Kennedy conundrum. Lincoln was elected to Congress in 1846, Kennedy in 1946. Lincoln became president in 1860, Kennedy in 1960. Lincoln's secretary was named Kennedy, Kennedy's was named Lincoln. Both were assassinated on a Friday by Southerners. John Wilkes Booth ran from the theatre and was caught in a warehouse. Lee Harvey Oswald ran from the warehouse and was caught in a theatre. Both Lincoln and Kennedy were succeeded by men named Johnson: Andrew Johnson was born in 1808, and Lyndon Johnson was born in 1908. Finally, both assassins, Booth and Oswald, were killed before their trials. Now that is uncanny.

• Amanda Foreman, *Spectator*, 16.5.98

★ ☆ ★

Lost gardens are legion. Cornwall alone has forfeited 25 magnificent ones in the last half-century. More great gardens, I suspect, have disappeared almost without trace than exist in the world today. Where are the countless gardens of Imperial Rome, with their copious basins and fountains, only half a dozen of which survive in any form? The enormous pleasure grounds, watered by the Nile and tended by a servile multitude, where the Pharaohs once walked, are now to be seen only in limestone low reliefs and tomb paintings. The wild ayatollahs of Persia not only neglect what is left of the *paradeisos* or elaborate hunting parks of the shahs, but would forcibly restrain anyone bold enough to try to rescue one.

Where are the apocalyptic Mughal gardens rising out of the surrounding deserts like mirages? Or the old Imperial gardens of the Sung and Ming dynasties? China indeed must be a garden restorer's heaven, for Mao's infamous cultural Revolution obliterated countless beautiful gardens, large and small, whose owners have been too scared to replant. There are lost pre-Columban gardens all along the high spine of Latin America, where Incas and Aztecs raised strange vegetables and fruits – flowers too, no doubt – on mossy terraces carefully guarded by granitic freestone walls. The Assyrian king Sennacherib, in the 8th century BC, had a garden of 16,000 plants linked by irrigation channels – the holes are still there, though all else has gone. A manuscript in the British Library shows another potentate, Ashurbanipal, lying down with his harem under the vine-covered trellises of his garden, while the heads of his conquered enemies hang from nearby orchard trees. Gone too, heads and all. The Greeks, especially the Stoics, lectured in an Athenian philosophy garden, also lost without trace. Nothing is left either of that opiary created by Pliny in his garden and described in one of his letters.

Oh that more could be done to bring back to breathing life the lost gardens of history! No art and science of archaeology, which always has a whiff of academic dust, can re-create the atmosphere of distant centuries so tenderly as a recovered garden, which brings us the scents and flavours of long, long ago, the languid hand trailing in the lily pond, the whispers and chuckles behind old box hedges, the glint of fountain spray on doublet and cloak, ruff and sword-hilt. A reborn garden is the best of all windows into the past.

• Paul Johnson, *Spectator*, 8.1.00

19 In The Beginning Was The Word

language and words

Broadcaster Robert Robinson has received an angry letter of complaint from a Radio 4 listener who heard him say on Brain of Britain that Jesus's first name was Reginald. 'Eventually, we worked out what had happened,' Robinson told the *Daily Express*. 'I had asked the question: What was Jeeves's first name?'

• This Life, *Sunday Times*, 20.11.99

★ ☆ ★

A Downing Street spokesman, the type that John Prescott, Deputy Leader and Minster of Transport, refers to as 'Faceless wonders' exacted his revenge yesterday at a Number Ten lobby briefing. 'Mr Prescott,' said the young whippersnapper, 'is in North Yorkshire today visiting whores.' A pause. 'That's Hawes in North Yorkshire.'

• Diary, *The Times*, 22.1.00

★ ☆ ★

For a cleric's son, Andreas Whittam Smith knows some very foul language. Indeed, visitors to his website might be a little taken aback. For there, hidden away among lots of interesting facts about obscure pieces of legislation dating back to 1952, Andreas, former editor of the *Independent*, has compiled a little list of some extraordinarily naughty words. He doesn't say they are his favourites but he does admit they are rude. He starts off slowly. 'Damn, hell, god, bloody, sod, tart, crap,' he exclaims, gradually building up – via 'shit', 'p*** off' and 'w*****', among many others – to 'f***'.

You'll notice that some asterisks have very kindly agreed to appear in this article, to protect the eyes of more sensitive readers. But Andreas, perhaps inured to such vulgarity after spending too long in the cinema, spells out all the words in full. And to think this man used to be in charge of a quality newspaper!

Perhaps a sentence or two of explanation are in order. (Perhaps blameless Mr Whittam Smith will sue if I don't come clean.) Andreas's list of rude words is in the name of science. He is the president of the British Board of Film Classification. And it is the BBFC website which prints all these swear words – 31 of them – in ascending order of vulgarity. The board is seeking partially to explain its licensing decisions and the role bad language plays in its decision to grant a particular film an 18 certificate instead of a 15. It is also looking for members of the public to give their verdict on the BBFC's swear word sensitivity.

There are five categories the BBFC uses: very mild (for example, damn), mild (bitch), moderate (shag), strong (f***) and very strong (the C-word). But naughty Andreas and his people have noticed that language changes. A word that was bloody ('very mild') rude in 1949 might not offend even the most insensitive dickhead ('mild') in 1999.

And because the BBFC brought out a similar list in July 1998, profanity-loving pop-pickers can follow which swear words have become more offensive, and which have become less offensive in the last year. So brace yourself for what's up and what's down in what we might call the Shit Parade if it weren't just a little too vulgar for a family newspaper.

Moving up the chart is bastard. Last year it stood as a paltry 'mild'. Now it's zoomed up to moderate, knocking bitch down from moderate to mild. Down, too, goes bloody (from mild to very mild), son of a bitch (mild to very mild) and crap (mild to very mild). Bollocks, though, has come on well since last year's rather unimpressive showing at mild. This year it's pushed through the moderate barrier along with whore and arsehole, both of which were, last year, merely mild. Sadly, fans of the words sod and hell will be disappointed that they have not moved above last year's very poor showing at very mild. But the winners are two words which have made new entries this year. They are certainly asterisk words, having not even been individually identified last year, when the BBFC merely referred elliptically to 'coarse' words, which it defined as 'stronger sexual swearwords'. But, hell, give a bloody, damn warm welcome to Andreas's rudest words in the world, singled out for the very first time in 1999 as 'very strong'. A round of applause, please, for...

The *Evening Standard* regrets that, due to a shortage of space, it is unable to print the rude words to which the author alludes above. Details of them are available on www.bbfc.co.uk, or in school playgrounds across London.

• Vincent Graf, *Evening Standard*, 3.11.99

★ ☆ ★

Coiners come and go, but coinages live on. What do you call somebody who continually applies his nose to the grindstone, eschews the distractions of fun and games and otherwise occupies himself with those moneymaking endeavours that make Jack a dull boy?

A workaholic, of course. But what did we call that addiction to work – that obsessive attachment to long hours and briefcases voluntarily stuffed with homework – before Wayne Oates, in a burst of linguistic innovation in 1968, titled an article in a parish magazine, On Being a 'Workaholic'?

It Takes All Sorts

We had no word for it. The language suffered from a gaping hole. The French had *burreau de travail*, 'work butcher', but not until this southern Baptist pastor from Louisville, Kentucky came up with his coinage could English speakers succinctly express themselves.

'I have dubbed this addiction of myself and my fellow ministers as workaholism,' Oates wrote, and later defined his term as 'the compulsion or the uncontrollable need to work incessantly.'

He based it, obviously, on alcoholic. In so doing, the coiner made a new suffix out of -oholic. But the question of spelling arises: if the suffix is adopted from alcoholic, why did Oates not spell his word workoholic?

I cannot ask him because Wayne Oates was one of those who died in the past year, remembered in history not so much for his 57 books and hundreds of published articles, but for his undisputed coinage of a necessary word. That's the way it goes in the word dodge; if you coin a good one, it becomes the lead of your obituary no matter what else you did.

• William Safire, *New York Times*, 8.1.200

★ ☆ ★

Santa has been banned from visiting a kindergarten in Victoria, Australia, after parents complained that he said 'ho, ho, ho' in an offensive manner. 'You can't please everybody,' said the kindergarten director.

• *Sunday Times*, 10.12.98

★ ☆ ★

Great Lies

The great and original lies of adulthood:

We must have lunch sometime.
The cheque is in the post.
It *really* suits you.

...and of childhood:

Everyone else has got one.
It was like that when I found it.
All my friends are going.

• P J Harford, Chippenham, letter to *The Times*, 21.1.00

★ ☆ ★

Has there been writing as coarse as this – as vulgar and violent, as otiosely overdone, as flushed with ugly, crimson tumescence – since the heyday of Mickey Spillane, whose PI, Mike Hammer, indifferently brutalised men, women and the English language?

This is a book whose very typography can give you an earache. Wolfe's style is the equivalent of a ghetto-blaster, or of the '20-inch speakers' which vomit heavy metal in one episode. Giving up the effort to use words expressively, he relies on amps – silently conjured up by tabloid capitals and inky italics – to hype his meaning. A telephone rings, and Wolfe mimics it: '*Trrrilll*'. (He does this 12 times because, I suppose, the phone goes on ringing.) Then a burglar alarm adds its voice: '*Brannnnng!*' (Now multiply by 17.) A fight between convicts begins with the pummelled loser squealing 'Awwwhhhhhh!' Then he screams 'AHHHHHHHHHHHHHHHHHHH!' Finally he screeches '*ahhhhhhhhhhhhhhh*'. This time there are fewer consonants and no exclamation mark, but the italics presumably vouch for an intenser agony.

During the earthquake, Wolfe audits the rumble of the tectonic plates, which say '*Thomp! Thomp! Thomp!*' while a siren vocalises '*woooo-woooo-woooo-woooo*'. Deluded by his own concrete poetry, he even ventures to rewrite symphonic music as typographic noise. The opening bars of Strauss's *Zarathustra*, which signal cosmic dawn in *2001* become '*BOOMboom-BOOMboomDAHdahhhhh*', while a passage from Beethoven's Sixth Symphony is rendered – without the aid of italic decibels – as 'Boom boom boom drizzle drizzle drizzle'.

• Peter Conrad, reviewing *A Man in Full* by Tom Wolfe, *Observer*, 25.10.98

★ ☆ ★

Like countless others, Smallweed was brought up to regard antidisestablishmentarianism as the longest word in the language. True, there were rival claims for floccinaucinihilipilification, but that was a joke word, damned by Chambers as facetious, whose only real purpose was to beat antidisestablishmentarianism's 28 letters. But now, it seems the long reign of antidisestablishmentarianism is over. A press release reaching the *Guardian* refers in the context of Bosnia to ethnotraumapsychopharmacology, which seems quite uncontrived, and is one letter longer than that great long word starting with A which I keep mentioning.

But before anyone claims any record for it, let Smallweed assert the claim of an even longer word which must plainly derive from it: ethnotraumapsychopharmacological (32). I recently came across a still longer word in the writings of Thomas Love Peacock, but that I think would have to be disqualified too, as merely Peacock playing about. It's tethrippharmatelasipedioploctypophilous, as in 'Oh, for goodness sake, stop being so tethrippharmatelasipedioploctypophilous, Kieron.' I have no idea what it means.

A pedant writes: It means being in a state of tethrippharmatelasipedioploctypophilousness. Surely everybody knows that.

• Smallweed, *Guardian*, 21.11.98

★ ☆ ★

Interesting little property, insurance and finance merger announced yesterday in Germany. A marriage has been arranged between Wuerttembergiesche Versicherungsbeteiligungsgesellschaft and Wuestenrot Beteiligungs. With just the slightest hint of desperation, the two companies say there's one outstanding item. A new name will be decided later.

• Observer, *Financial Times*, 4.11.98

★ ☆ ★

'How was the skiing?' I asked a friend. 'Huge,' was his answer. This was a new one on me. The more usual word these days for anything that gives more than pleasure would be 'large', as in 'he's having it large'. It could be that, in the way of these things, 'large' is already losing out to the need for something stronger.

Until recently, the usual answer to such questions would have been 'great'. This does not, of course, mean that 'huge' will ever entirely supplant the earlier word. 'Did you look great in '98?' was the headline on an end-of-year article in the *Sunday Telegraph*. The correct response to 'Do I look all right?' is still 'You look great', not 'You look huge'. But I expect 'huge', if not 'large', to gain currency in the coming years.

The trouble with 'great' is that its credibility rating is wearing thin. It was fine in its early days when it stopped being just a measure of size and began to stand for something fine and noble as well, but that was a very long time ago. It can now be as perfunctory as you like – an acknowledgement of small favours, a sign of agreement, or perhaps a way of conveying sarcasm ('I'm afraid I wiped that tape.' – 'Oh, great.').

Meanwhile fashions come and go. 'Monstrous' and 'monstrously' had a good long innings until they fell out of favour in the late 19th century, and are now strictly reserved for serious purposes.

'Hugely', on the other hand, looks as though it will run. Its resonances remain strong and healthy. Even today the word is capable of evoking impressive, almost threatening bulk, something that 'massive' has long since lost as a result of its gross overuse, first by the politically committed ('massive' injustice etc), then by ordinary journalists.

In due course, 'huge' will follow 'great' and 'massive' in a limbo of discarded qualifiers, with no power to evoke anything much. But it won't happen yet.

• Nicholas Bagnall, in the *Independent on Sunday*, 10.1.99

★ ☆ ★

A row has broken out in the world of fine wines. In a BBC documentary, *Vintners' Tales*, Mr Michael Broadbent, director of Christie's fine wine department, is asked why he never goes to the same wine tasting as Serena Sutcliffe, the supremo of Sotheby's international wine department. He replies: 'Really, I find her haughty and rather nose-in-the-air. The word, if you really want the word, is pretentious.'

Pretentious, *elle?* Of all the words you might expect a wine expert to use in condemnation of another wine expert, 'pretentious' is the last. For pretentiousness comes with the territory. It's a requirement of the job. An unpretentious wine connoisseur would be as much use as a surreptitious town crier.

Enemies of Ms Sutcliffe can point to some spectacular feats of adjectival fireworks in her attempts to encapsulate the glory of crushed grape juice. She is fond of words such as *monumental, fabulous, incandescent, mythical, eternal, immense, archetypal, awe-inspiring, majestic* and 'grandiose, in the French sense' when describing upmarket drinks.

In the last year's auction of Andrew Lloyd Webber's wine collection she identified the flavours of 'jammy wonder', 'glorious toasted lime', 'hawthorn and honey' and 'the Cairo spice bazaar' in a number of expensive *premiers crus classés* clarets. To her phenomenal, hair-trigger sensory arsenal, the 1959 Domaine de la Romanée Conti Burgundy was 'rich coffee and undergrowth on the nose, cocoa on the palate'.

You may, like Mr Broadbent, find this stuff hard to take. You may decide, like him, that 'the word...is pretentious'. And I would reply: so what? What's *wrong* with being pretentious?

What, for example, is the alternative to Ms Sutcliffe's synaesthetic deductions? To say (as Mr Broadbent once said of a supermarket *vin ordinaire*) that it's 'an ordinary, straight-forward red colour and smells vaguely of wine'? Give me Ms Sutcliffe any day. To those who poo-pooh E M Forster's reading of Beethoven's Fifth Symphony as an uprising of goblins against their Creator, I'd say it represents a more coherent response to the music than saying you like the tunes. To people who laugh at the Millennium Dome as not just over-priced but 'pretentious', I'd say that's precisely why I love it – because it combines with such insouciance the qualities of biblical crown of thorns, royal crown and crown roast of lamb.

'Pretentious' is a word we hurl too readily at human attempts to see transcendent things in the everyday. If my neighbour claims to detect the odour of Kirov ballet tights in a bottle of Chilean merlot, if my daughter sees the shadow of mortality in a melting ice-lolly, or if I claim that a three-line haiku by Lao-tzu is the finest expression of love in the history of poetry, we may all be guilty of pretension – but at least we tried.

For the enemies of pretension are far worse than its exponents. We detect pretension in others when we dislike their claims to a sensitivity that's greater than our own. We think they're just pretending a response. They're faking a rapture we don't (or can't) share. They see stars where we see mud. They are either lucky bastards or they're posey charlatans. Let's agree it must be the latter.

But it's the *courting* of pretension that makes life worthwhile. If we like or love or hate something, if we feel joy or pain or sorrow and look for some metaphorical correlative of it in the outside world, let us indulge ourselves as we like without this dull, prosaic condemnation. We may be imprecise or overly colourful, we may make idiots of ourselves, but at least we expressed it, whether the result was an over-excited tasting note or Chartres Cathedral.

For without the occasional foray into grandiosity (in the English sense), affectation or even vanity, life would be ghastly. Without pretension there would be no fine art, no poetry, no architecture, no advertising slogans, no religion, no Zen, no couture fashion, no speeches, no metaphors, hardly any pop lyrics, no satire. The world would be a place of cold sense, precise description, modest utterance, a grim calibration of external facts, a sterile dystopia of functional buildings and sensible clothing. And all the wine would taste just of wine.

• John Walsh, *Independent*, 30.9.98

★ ☆ ★

Clichés, damn then, continue to infuriate me. The trouble with clichés, of course, is that they are so useful. A cliché's felicity in its original context was so remarkable that the phrase has become over-used and stereotyped.

Questions can become clichés. 'How do you feel?' is not only over-used and banal, but now has the effect of hardly ever being relevant. There are rare occasions when the question needs to be broadcast, and the reply is worth hearing. Often, the question is edited out of a report. But the fury generated by asking, say, a seaman who staggers ashore after being rescued from a 24-hour ordeal in an open boat, 'How do you feel?' is justified: I am always astonished by the courtesy of our interviewees. That seaman will probably say something cheerful, like, 'Oh, OK, thanks.'

I do not have that kind of self-control. Perhaps my antipathy began years ago in hospital. After an operation, I lay in bed, inside a plastic bag, tubes into both arms, another coming out of my nose, being regularly pumped full of painkillers, beginning to realize what hell and havoc injury can cause. Someone came to see me, determined in his effervescent Welsh way, to cheer me up. He stood at the side of the bed – I could just make him out through the haze – and asked: 'How do you feel, then? In *yourself* I mean.'

• Alan Protheroe, *Listener*, 3.3.83

★ ☆ ★

A meeting, in the definition coined by the satirical novelist Vladimir Voinovich, is an occasion when people gather together, some to say what they do not think, and others not to say what they really do.

• Geoffrey Hoskins, from Reith Lectures 1988, *Listener*, 10.11.88

★ ☆ ★

The more you think about it, the less attractive becomes the idea of world English. The French rightly hate it. In my own lifetime French was still the language of diplomacy. Even as the Cold War got going, respectable newspapers still referred to M. Molotov, M. Vishinsky and even M. Stalin. Why should not French have remained the diplomatic language, given that it was the French who virtually invented modern diplomacy? To have waged the Cold War in French might have introduced useful intellectual standards, a superior rationality. Instead we fell into the shrill language of moralistic abuse that the Americans have always found congenial, and that has now become normal for all of us.

The attempt to detach language from culture is not new. An 18th-century bishop, John Wilkins, tried to devise a universal language based on a scientific description of the world. He translated the Lord's Prayer into this language. It did not catch on – any more than did his proposal for men to be transported to the moon by flocks of geese.

World English is the worst thing that could happen to us. It will mean that the English of England and the British Isles will come to be seen as just one dialect among many – without even the special status that Tuscany has in Italy. We will be engulfed by computer-speak, international science-speak, Unesco-speak, and international-business lingo. We will be in an even worse position than the French in their struggle against Franglais – for French is, at least, clearly a distinct language. Given our current insouciance towards our own high culture (so different from the robust self-pride of the French) we will have deprived ourselves of the chief bulwarks against the flood.

• John Casey, *Spectator*, 1.1.00

★ ☆ ★

Universities, for all their pretensions, generally have a lamentable record of giving in, particularly where free speech is concerned, to governments, pressure groups, rioting students and assorted wowsers, and American universities in this respect are usually worse than most. So when I learned from the *New York Times* that one of them – and Berkeley, at that – was under attack on a matter of principle, I felt that I would not have long to wait before I got the news that the authorities had surrendered.

It may yet happen; but I have to report that so far Berkeley is not only standing firm on its battlements, with the drawbridge raised, but is energetically pouring boiling oil on to the heads of the besiegers, accompanied by cries of derision.

It began when the vice-chancellor received a complaint from an official (a lawyer, of course) in the Office of Civil Rights, which comes under the Education Department of the state government of California. The complaint was levelled against the directory of courses offered by Berkeley, at first blush an unlikely candidate for offences against civil rights. Had Berkeley, I asked myself, been offering tuition in lynching, in the daubing of anti-semitic slogans, in the framing of those with unacceptable political opinions?

Nothing so trivial; the complaint was directed at references, in the course calendar, to 'mankind', 'manpower' and 'man-made'. The official (hereinafter known as The Pest) demanded the removal of such words and their replacement by words of indeterminate gender, such as 'staff development' for 'manpower' (The Pest seems to be illiterate as well as impudent), 'human-produced' for 'man-made', and 'the human species' or 'human populations' for 'mankind' (which would do wonders for Goldsmith's epitaph on Burke – 'Who, born for the Universe, narrow'd his mind, And to party gave up what was meant for the human species' – and even more for Donne's 'Any man's death diminishes me, because I am involved in human populations').

Vive la difference! For what is behind this wearisome nonsense has nothing to do with discrimination against women. It is part of one of the worst of all the plagues of our world, the desire to pretend that all human beings are, or if they are not should be obliged to become, identical. Since inequality is built permanently into the human gene structure – so that most of us, for instance, could never run a mile in four minutes or play the violin like Sir Yehudi Menuhin (however long and hard we trained and practised) – and since the people who direct the movement I have described cannot (for reasons still obscure) bear to face that elementary truth, those who wish to push their mad and odious view forward must with one hand pretend that our inability to rival Sebastian Coe or Sir Yehudi is due only to our environment, and with the other find instances in which the names of things can be made equivalent if the things themselves cannot.

It is this tide that has swept over a word like 'elite' and changed its meaning from something admirable to something hateful; the same noisome sea has drowned vital educational principles; driftwood from our taxation system bobs in the same flood. And because men and women are different, it follows that those who want to turn us all into helots of a totalitarian and illusory equality just do what they can to deny the existence, let alone the nature, of that difference. And since they cannot do so in reality, they try to do it in words.

• Bernard Levin, *The Times*, 19.7.85

* ☆ *

English as She is Mis-spoke

In a Vienna hotel: 'In case of fire, do your utmost to alarm the porter.'

In a Greek tailor shop: 'Order your summers suit. Because is big rush cunt, we will execute customers in strict rotation.'

In a Hong Kong supermarket: 'For your convenience, we recommend courteous, efficient self-service.'

In a Hong Kong dentist: 'Teeth extracted by the latest Methodists.'

In a Bucharest hotel lobby: 'The lift is being fixed for the next day. During that time we regret you will be unbearable.'

In a Hong Kong tailor shop: 'Ladies may have fits upstairs.'

In a Roman clinic: 'Specialist in women and other diseases.'

In a hotel in an Austrian ski resort: 'Not to perambulate the corridors in the hours of repose in the boots of ascension.'

• Business translations quoted in *Toronto Globe and Mail*, 15.4.98, spotter: Brendan Joseph O'Byrne. Quoted by Victor Lewis-Smith in *Private Eye*

★ ☆ ★

If we all spoke a common language, things might work more smoothly – but with less scope for amusement. Consider this warning to Tokyo motorists some years ago:

'At the rise of the hand of the policeman, stop rapidly. Do not pass him or otherwise disrespect him.

'When a passenger of the foot heave in sight, tootle the horn. Trumpet at him melodiously at first, but if he still obstacles your passage, then tootle him with vigour.

'Beware of greasy corner where lurk skid demon. Cease step on, approach slowly, round cautiously, resume step on gradually.'

A hotel in Yugoslavia put this notice on its doors: 'Guests should announce the abandonment of theirs rooms before 12 o'clock, emptying the room at the latest until 14 o'clock, for the use of the room before 5 at the arrival or after the 16 o'clock at the departure, will be billed as one night more.

• Bill Bryson, *Readers Digest*, Sept. 1992, quoting from his book *The Mother Tongue*

★ ☆ ★

English may be spoken all over the world but sometimes it suffers in translation with hilarious results. We know what they meant to say, but somehow it came out all wrong when foreign hotel managers, restaurateurs and shop-owners put up what they thought were helpful signs. They include:

'Do not use the diving board when the swimming pool is empty.' (Swimming pool in Sri Lanka)

'To call room service, please open the door and call room service.' (Istanbul hotel)

'It is forbidden to steal hotel towels. If you are a person to do such thing please not read this.' (Tokyo hotel)

'It is forbidden to enter a woman even a foreigner if dressed as a man.' (Bangkok temple)

• *The Sun,* 13.11.92; and *Evening Standard,* 3.9.97 reviewing *Please Take Advantage of the Chambermaid and Other Silly Signs* (Michael O'Mara Books)

★ ☆ ★

It is absolutely monstrous the way people nowadays go about saying things against one behind one's back that are absolutely and entirely true.

• Oscar Wilde, *A Woman of No Importance*

★ ☆ ★

Oratory, phrases, the evocative power of verbal symbols must not be despised, for these have been one of the chief means of uniting the United States and keeping it united.

• S W Brogan

★ ☆ ★

Oratory is the art of making a loud noise sound like a deep thought.

★ ☆ ★

A speech is like a love affair. Any fool can start it, but to end it requires considerable skill.

• Anon

★ ☆ ★

The limits of my language are the limits of my world.

• Wittgenstein

★ ☆ ★

Here are some new academic words that have been sent in to me. They have been collected over the last few years from academic papers, seminars, and more general sources. Some of them serve good purposes, but are nevertheless plain ugly. Others arise from the manic desire to 'ize' any nouns found loitering. Some are the products of disturbed minds. It is interesting to note that a lot of 'izing' occurs in linguistics and phonetics. It is a disgrace and a tragedy that academic specialities dealing with the English language have become so inaccessible to its owners.

Concertize (to give a concert: Canadian); co-ordinatize (to impose a co-ordinate system); Multiculturalism Minister (Canadian); procedurealized/procedureing, lexicalize; bourgeoisification; discretize; Christianize; diphthongization; pharyngealization; intervocalically; hypothesization; fuzzification (from fuzzy logic); trainability; intercomprehensibility; creolization; glottalization; labialization; velarization; dealphabetize; alphabeticizer; binarization; calculatable; decontextualized; pidginization; associationism; dichotomizer; rhotacization; psychologism; maximalistically, minimalistically; particularization; grammaticalize; jargonise; communicology; parallelization; prioritized; fricativized; systematicity; historicist; routinized; euthing (performing euthanasia); objectification; comprehensivization; recognology; cognitronics; tailorable; summating; electronical; casualize; Godelization; chaology (the mathematical study of chaos); complexification; pressurization; spontain (verb: a favourite of Jonathan Miller); diagrammed; mechanizability; collocationally.

• Philip Howard, *The Times*, 14.9.85

★ ☆ ★

One of my philosophers has got me into minor trouble with the censor. The other day I did an interview with *Sky Books*. A genial presenter asked me to tell him about the philosopher Montaigne and how he might help us over some everyday ailments. I explained that Montaigne believed our societies to be afflicted by terrible prudery about the body and that the solution was to start calling a spade a spade. In Montaigne's day, at least, representative stories and images did not identify virtue and grace with the human body. Montaigne knew one woman who was so embarrassed by her digestive processes that she insisted on eating behind a curtain. A neighbour of his became impotent during love-making and, believing himself to suffer from a unique curse, cut off his penis and sent it to the lady, as Montaigne put it, 'to atone for his offence'. Pictures of kings and ladies did not encourage one to think of these eminent souls breaking wind or making love. So Montaigne felt it important to fill out the picture in blunt, beautiful French: 'Au plus eslevé throne du monde si ne sommes assis que sus nostre cul,' he wrote, which Montaigne's superlative modern translator, the Revd Professor Michael Screech, translated as: 'Upon the highest throne in the world, we are seated, still, upon our arses.' And 'Les Roys et les philosophes fientent, et les dames aussi,' 'Kings and philosophers shit; and so do ladies.'

The man from *Sky Books* seemed genuinely impressed by Montaigne's argument. So it was somewhat disconcerting to tune in to Sky for the books programme and discover that the producers must have had second thoughts (and were more prudish than a reverend), for I found myself saying, 'Upon the highest throne in the world, we are seated, still upon our *beep*' and 'Kings and philosophers *beep;* and so do ladies.' How might Montaigne have responded to *Sky Books*? With his customary good humour and politeness, he would probably have repeated what he said in one of his *Essays*: 'The genital activities of mankind are so natural, so necessary and so right; what have they done to make us never dare to mention them without embarrassment and to exclude them from serious orderly conversation? We are not afraid to utter the words *kill, thieve,* or *betray*; but those others we only dare to mutter through our teeth.'

• Alain de Botton, *Spectator*, 22.4.00

20 Take Two Spoonfuls Of Laughter Daily

laughter and humour

Clerihews

These verses usually flow naturally enough but are distinguished by the wit or surprise of the last line. The first Clerihew is credited to Edmund Clerihew Bentley who at sixteen wrote the first one.

Sir Humphrey Davy,
Detested gravy.
He lived in the odium
Of having discovered sodium.

Other famous Clerihews are:

The moustache of Hitler
Could hardly be littler,
Was the thought that kept recurring
To Field Marshal Goering.

Frederick the Great
Became king at twenty-eight.
In a fit of amnesia
He invaded Silesia.

It Takes All Sorts

What I like about Clive
Is that he is no longer alive.
There is a great deal to be said
About being dead.

Houdini
Was teeny.
No one could bind him
They couldn't even find him.

Nietzsche
Used to write down every fietzsche
Of the human psyche
Cryche!

Nostradamus
Never wore pyjamas.
'What's the use?' he would say
'When the world might not last the night anyway.'

* ☆ *

Scientists have proved that laughing is good for you. Cognitive Psychologist Mariana Funes suggests practising laughing on your own – or with a group of friends. Dr Robert Renshaw of the Happiness Centre agrees: 'The practice of daily, unreasonable laughter [laughing, for no apparent reason] can become a habit, like brushing your teeth. It can alter your mood and your outlook on life. You just have to be willing.'

Try these five exercises at home with a friend or partner. You might feel a bit self-conscious at first, but you should feel better afterwards:

1 Find a word that makes you laugh and repeat it to each other in silly voices.

2 Laugh for no reason at all for at least a minute.
3 Walk around the room, trying to impersonate different emotional states: the angry walk, the grumpy walk or the happy walk.
4 Learn to give yourself and others permission to laugh for no reason at all.
5 Do something that makes you laugh every day, or make sure you speak to a friend who always makes you laugh.

• Verity Owen, *Daily Telegraph*, 16.6.00

★ ☆ ★

How much do you laugh at work? I bet you'll say you don't laugh much. Work, after all, is not particularly funny. Indeed, the sight of a few colleagues wearing those idiotic red noses on Comic Relief Day was enough to remind most sensible people just how unfunny work really is.

But if someone actually measured how often you laugh in the office, you might be surprised. We laugh a lot more often than we think we do. Laughter at work has precious little to do with being amusing, with joking, or with fun of any sort. It has everything to do with office politics. Which is to say it is all about power.

Think of the Royal Family. These unfunny, uptight people actually make people laugh more easily than the professional comedians Rory Bremner and Dawn French put together. The Queen only has to make the lamest pleasantry on an official visit and everyone convulses. They laugh not because they are remotely amused but because they are nervous. She is more powerful than they are.

The same thing happens every day in offices everywhere. When your boss makes a joke, you laugh without thinking. The more senior and the more scary the boss, the greater your mirth.

It is not that you are a sycophant, it is that you understand the system.

Making a joke yourself is a much riskier matter, as I have often found. You listen to your seniors' jokes and falsely conclude that general jocularity is welcomed. You make a joke. Everyone ignores it. Disaster. We need to understand 'humour' better at work. The flatter the hierarchy, the more complicated things are. A good rule of thumb is that if people listen to you and laugh at your jokes, you are going somewhere. If not, then you're not.

• Lucy Kellaway, *Financial Times*, 15.3.99

★ ☆ ★

In 1954 Milton Shulman set a competition in the *New Statesman* in which competitors were asked to compose a postcard from a friend on holiday 'Wishing you were here' that made you thankful you were still at home. The following were amongst the winners:

☆

Peace, perfect peace! The monastery is 15,000 feet above sea-level – incredible views on clear days. Some of the Paying Guests troubled with headaches and nose-bleeding because of the height. But I never felt better.

Strict monastic routine for all! No talking except for 45 minutes after morning service (4 a.m.) and then only Latin. Latin a real living language here, not the fossilized Ciceronian stuff we learned. I help a party of lay brothers who are building a new chapel on an adjacent peak – quarrying our own stone. It is immense fun and really rewarding – and it keeps us warm.

No, they don't make liqueurs. How could they at this height?

HJR

☆

Arrived Rome after good journey from Genoa – averaged over 40 m.p.h. Bus running well and managed to touch 105 in places. Had a slight prang in Paris but no vital damage to car (touch wood!) I am OK apart from a couple of broken ribs. Now pushing on to Naples Brindisi and then hope to get a half day in at Venice. After that will press on to Belgrade and Athens, but must step on the gas to get back home by 29th. Food a bit grim and the foreign types ditto, but the Wops marvellous with the bus. Having great time and wish you were here.

Ben Ellison

☆

Did near-vertical North Face of Unchrlichefrauspitz today. Wet rock, ice patches and strong winds made route very amusing. Interesting pitch up chimney with smooth walls and 10-ton loose chock-stone. Jock led up slabs of exposed arete, where we had snack of dry schwartzbrot – Jock had lost rest of food in chimney! Magnificent series of thunder-clouds swept over from Zugspitz during very severe last pitch. Amusing descent in storm. Look forward to interesting ice-work tomorrow. Do hope you can come on to us from Juan-les-Pin next week.

J E Wardroper

★ ☆ ★

Invitations You Wish You'd Never Received

I hope you don't mind squeezing in with the labrador in the back. He's not nearly as fierce as he looks.

We've got lots of exciting things planned for the weekend so be sure and bring your sleeping-bag.

Not a bit out of my way. I'll drop you off at the top of the High Street. It's the best place to get taxis after midnight.

Invitation to a party: Everyone's dressing in purple.

You've accepted on the phone an invitation for dinner and then your host tells you: 'It'll be a family dinner. Just us, the little ones and Henry's old German tutor.'

Sheila's into Elizabethan cooking at the moment so I hope you won't mind some larks' wings pie and our own home-made mead.

• BBC Stop The Week, November 1980

★ ☆ ★

She has a penetrating sort of laugh. Rather like a train going into a tunnel.

• P G Wodehouse

★ ☆ ★

Passenger at a bar on the *Titanic*: 'I asked for ice, but this is ridiculous!'

★ ☆ ★

An American professor visiting a museum in Wales asked one of the attendants what was the age of the huge skeleton of a dinosaur at the end of one of the galleries. 'Oh, that skeleton is eighty-six million and six years old.'

'Oh!' said the professor, impressed by such meticulous accuracy. 'Can you tell me how you know its age so precisely?'

'Well,' said the attendant, 'I've been working for this museum for six years and that dinosaur's skeleton was eighty-six million years old when I first came here.'

★ ☆ ★

Life does not cease to be funny when people die any more than it ceases to be serious when people laugh.

• George Bernard Shaw

★ ☆ ★

Right-wing American humorist P J O'Rourke was accused of bad taste on Tuesday night after a remark about General Pinochet's victims. 'Pinochet did kill a whole bunch of people,' he declared at a Royal Overseas League meeting to discuss his new book *Eat the Rich*. 'But then again they were bad people.' Most of the audience laughed but one woman complained: 'It's not funny that people died.' 'Ma'am, I want to tell you something about humour. It isn't a nice thing. When a kitten plays with a ball of wool it is only funny when it strangles itself.' My sentiments precisely.

• Brutus, *Daily Express*, 4.12.98

★ ☆ ★

It was the season to be funny. Only nobody ever is. They bear down on you, those vile bods at Christmas and New Year parties, eyes exhibiting what they believe to be a waggish twinkle and you know to be the type of ugly glaze you get only on a winter alocoholiday. They open their mouths despoiled by rows of putrid, foaming cavities. It is then that the dreadful realisation comes upon one that they are about to tell a joke.

I hate laughter – it causes laughter lines. It contorts the face into a shape and consistency resembling that of a squashed potato. It ain't no laughing matter. Grinning too often ages people more surely and more swiftly than lying on tinfoil under a Caribbean sun for eight months of the year.

The most attractive facial expressions, on the other hand, are repose and gravity, even sorrow. Nothing makes a woman or a man more winning – and worth the wear of winning – than a minor tragedy; that hint of melancholy Victoriana – you know: From sport to sport they hurry me to stifle my regret / And when they win a smile from me, they think that I forget.

• Petronella Wyatt, *Spectator*, 2.1.99

★ ☆ ★

On the subject of hunchbacks, when Quasimodo died, the biggies of Notre Dame had a terrible time finding a replacement. No one could duplicate Quasimodo's bell-ringing. Then a poor wretch without arms came to the archbishop and asked for the job. 'But how will you manage it, my son?' asked His Eminence. The cripple motioned for the priest to follow him, then took a long run and hit the bell at full speed with his forehead. A heavenly sound.

Maybe it was blind luck, thought the archbishop. He asked the cripple to do it again. Same thing. A flying start, and dingggg, dongggg; a crowd started to gather below. 'Quasimodo lives!' someone cried. 'You've got the job,' said the priest. 'Hooray!' shouted the cripple and began to jump with joy. So much so he fell off the steeple and crashed sickeningly below. The archbishop, horrified, went down to give him the last rites. 'Did you know the poor man?' asked the people. 'No, but his face rings a bell,' answered His Eminence.

• Taki, *Spectator*, 13.5.00

21 Dying Is Easier Than Living

life, death, last words and epitaphs

I would not wish eternal life on my worst enemy.

• Quentin Crisp, quoted in *Daily Telegraph* obituary, 22.11.99

★ ☆ ★

'Why shouldn't a man enjoy his own death?' said Terence Rattigan to the actor, Keith Baxter. 'After all, it's the last amusement left.'

• Charles Spencer reviewing Michael Darlow's *Terence Rattigan*, *Sunday Telegraph*, 15.1.00

★ ☆ ★

What would it pleasure me to have my throat cut
With diamonds? or to be smothered
With Cassia? Or to be shot to death with pearls?
I know that death hath ten thousand several doors
For men to take their exits; and 'tis found
They go on such strange geometric hinges
You may open them both ways: anyway, for heaven's sake,
So I were out of your whispering.

• From *The Duchess of Malfi* by John Webster (1580?–1625?)

★ ☆ ★

As I gave my grandfather's gravestone a good stare, I recalled his last words, delivered as he lay dying in a hospital bed. 'It's like that, is it?' – said with a weak smile, after the doctor had asked if he wanted to go home. I imagine most last words are non-sequiturs, or frightened pieties, or overly polished witticisms. The problem with thinking about your last words in advance, though, is that you might not get them out in time or, worse, you might mis-time it and then have to follow them up with a sheepish, 'Could you pass me a glass of water?'

Conrad Hilton, the man who founded the hotels, had a good last line: 'Leave the shower curtain on the inside of the tub.' And Lady Astor's is rather endearing. Regaining consciousness briefly to find herself surrounded by her entire family she said: 'Am I dying, or is this my birthday?' The last words of Dominique Bouhours, the French Jesuit grammarian who worked endlessly to promote a high standard of correctness and purity in the French language, were doubtless premeditated, but they are no less charming for that: 'I am about to – or I am going to – die; either expression is used.'

Historians now believe that the most famous last words ever spoken, those of George V, may not have been accurately recorded. *The Times* reported that they were 'How goes the Empire?' but everyone knew they were really 'Bugger Bognor' (before his death, his doctor assured him he would soon recover and be able to holiday at Bognor Regis). Recently, though, the diary of the attending physician was published; it states that after being given a shot of morphine, the King's last words were 'God damn you!' I think I prefer those.

But the prize for the most wistful last words should go to the playwright William Saroyan. 'Everybody has got to die, but I had always belived an exception would be made in my case.'

• Nigel Farndale, *Sunday Telegraph* Magazine, 25.2.2001

* ☆ *

It was a job to die for, requiring little more than a talent for standing around, but only six applicants auditioned yesterday for the post of a knife-thrower's assistant.

Managers at the Cottle & Austen Circus have been trying to fill the post for the almost a year after the previous occupant was promoted to be a vampire. In response to a Job Centre advertisement four women and two men turned up to stand against a 3 ft high board while the knife-thrower, Jayde Hanson, hurled steel blades in their direction at 60 mph.

On her application form, Alison Ewen said that she would be good at the job because she was a cook and so used to being around cutlery. Victoria Brown celebrated her nineteenth birthday by auditioning and described the experience as exhilarating. Gail Lawrence, 19, said: 'It wasn't as bad as it seemed.'

Before he began throwing, Mr Hanson assured them all that he had been practising his art since he was ten and had never inflicted a major injury on anyone, although he did cut a former girlfriend three times. She later left him.

• Gillian Harris, *The Times*, 13.8.2000

★ ☆ ★

In the year of 1929, I spent several weeks in the hospital X, in the fifteenth arrondissement of Paris. The clerks put me through the usual third-degree at the reception desk, and indeed I was kept answering questions for some 20 minutes before they would let me in. For some days past I had been unequal to translating Reaumur into Fahrenheit, but I know that my temperature was round about 103°, and by the end of the interview I had some difficulty in standing on my feet. At my back a resigned little knot of patients, carrying bundles done up in coloured handkerchiefs, waited their turn to be questioned.

After the questioning came the bath, a compulsory routine for all newcomers, apparently, just as in prison or the workhouse. My clothes were taken away, and after I had sat shivering for some minutes in five inches of warm water I was given a linen nightshirt and a short, blue flannel dressing-gown – no slippers, they had none big enough for me, they said – and led me out into the open air.

This was a night in February and I was suffering from pneumonia. The ward we were going to was 200 yards away and it seemed that to get to it you had to cross the hospital grounds. Someone stumbled in front of me with a lantern. The gravel path was frosty underfoot and the wind whipped the nightshirt round my bare calves. When we got into the ward, I was aware of a strange feeling of familiarity whose origin I did not succeed in pinning down till later in the night. It was a long, rather low, ill-lit room, full of murmuring voices and with three rows of beds surprisingly close together. There was a foul smell, faecal and yet sweetish.

My right hand neighbour was a little, red-haired cobbler with one leg shorter than the other, who used to announce the death of any other patient (this happened a number of times) by whistling to me, exclaiming: 'Numero 43!' (or whatever it was) and flinging his arms above his head.

About a dozen beds away from me was Numero 57, a cirrhosis of the liver case, a man about 60. Everyone in the ward knew him by sight because he was sometimes the subject of a medical lecture. On two afternoons a week, a tall, grave, black-bearded doctor would lecture in the ward to a party of students, and on more than one occasion old Numero 57 was wheeled on a sort of trolley into the middle of the ward, where the doctor would roll back his nightshirt, dilate with his fingers a huge, flabby protuberance on the man's belly – the diseased liver, I suppose – and explain solemnly that this was a disease attributable to alcoholism, common in the wine-drinking countries.

As usual, he neither spoke to his patient nor gave him a smile, a nod or any kind of recognition. While he talked, he would hold the wasted body beneath his two hands, sometimes giving it a gentle roll to and fro, in just the attitude of a woman handling a rolling-pin.

One morning, my cobbler neighbour woke me by plucking at my pillow before the nurses arrived. 'Numero 57!' – he flung his arms about his head. There was a light in the ward, enough to see by. I could see old Numero 57 lying crumpled upon his side, his face sticking out over the side of the bed, and towards me. He had died some time during the night; nobody knew when. When the nurses came, they received the news of his death indifferently and went about their work. After a long time, an hour or more, two other nurses marched in abreast like soldiers, and knotted the corpse up in the sheets, but it was not removed till some time later.

Meanwhile, in the better light, I had had time for a good look at Numero 57. Indeed, I lay on my side to look at him. Curiously enough, he was the first dead European I had seen. I had seen dead men before, but always Asiatics and usually people who had died violent deaths. Numero 57's eyes were still open, his mouth also open, his small face contorted into an expression of agony. What most impressed me however was the whiteness of his face. It had been pale before, but now it was little darker than the sheets.

As I gazed at the tiny, screwed-up face, it struck me that this disgusting piece of refuse, waiting to be carted away and dumped on a slab in the dissecting room, was an example of 'natural' death, one of the things you pray for in the Litany.

There you are, then, I thought, that's what is waiting for you, 20, 30, 40 years hence; that is how the lucky ones die, the ones who live to be old. One wants to live, indeed one only stays alive by virtue of the fear of death, but I think it's better to die violently and not too old.

- From 'How the Poor Die' from the *Complete Works of George Orwell*, ed. Peter Davison © the estate of the late Sonia Brownell Orwell. Quoted in *Observer* Review, 16.1.00

★ ☆ ★

Today I buried my father-in-law at sea. Buried is probably not the word for it. There was no body. What we did was cast his ashes to the four winds.

I've never seen a person's ashes before. I suppose I'd unthinkingly assumed that 'ashes' was only a way of speaking, that what we burn down to is some sort of odoriferous powder, finer and sweeter-perfumed than talcum, and somehow still animated by soul. But we don't. We make the same sort of ash as a bonfire makes. Grey and grainy and unspiritual. Plenty of it, too. A whole plastic flaskful, which can take a fair bit of shaking out. Especially if your hands aren't steady.

I've never fancied being burned myself. I'm too worried about the possibility of a mistake. Imagine lying inside that highly flammable wooden lozenge and listening to it crackle while you're still alive, still able to hear the congregation singing 'Jerusalem'. Imagine the condition of your mind. Illogical, I know, given that you can be buried alive just as easily. But then I've never fancied the soil option either. Earth, water, air, fire – let those who were happy to live in the elements, die in the elements. You're either an earth's diurnal course man or you're not. I'm not. I keep hoping I can hold out long enough for someone to discover some new and more suitable medium for my expiry. Something less natural. Evaporation through abstruse sentence, say. Interment in metaphor.

Scatter me in words, O my beloved.

• Howard Jacobson, *Independent*, 31.8.98

★ ☆ ★

I'm not afraid to die, I just don't want to be there when it happens.

• Woody Allen

★ ☆ ★

The sawn-off head of Billy Moseley, a 36 year old small-time crook, was kept in a deep freeze for possibly three years, a London coroner's court was told yesterday. Professor James Cameron said there was no evidence of death.

• *Daily Telegraph*, Oct 1977

★ ☆ ★

Lord Finchley tried to mend the electric light
Himself. It struck him dead: and serve him right,
It is the business of the wealthy man
To give employment to the artisan.

★ ☆ ★

Here lies the body of Sir John Guise
Nobody laughs and nobody cries,
Where his soul is, and how it fares,
Nobody knows and nobody cares.

• Anon

★ ☆ ★

It Takes All Sorts

An old man on his death-bed confided to his family that he had had lots of trouble in his life, most of which had never happened.
• Winston Churchill

* ☆ *

Sir, the letter on 'Guillotine horror' reminds me of beheadings for murder and drug trafficking I witnessed when resident in Saudi Arabia. On each occasion, a heavy, razor-sharp sword was wielded so expertly that the slice took but an instant.

On discussing the matter with a surgeon friend who was briefly a locum in Jeddah, I remarked that the cut was so swift that the condemned man could not have felt anything. He countered by saying that, under medical conditions, one retains consciousness for two or three minutes after the blood supply to the head is cut off. This indicates that, unless rendered unconscious by hitting the ground, a person's severed head remains sentient after the sentence has been executed.

A police officer who occasionally presided at executions subsequently confirmed this. He told me that if the head is picked up too soon it employs its only remaining defence mechanism – it bites!

• N F Parker, letter to the *Daily Telegraph*, 10.6.00. (The letter he refers to told how a number of felons sentenced to die had been asked to blink if they felt anything after their lopped heads fell into the basket. A number of the dead had duly blinked.)

22 Marriage Is A Sentence Not A Word

love and marriage

If you're afraid of loneliness, do not marry.

• Anton Chekhov

★ ☆ ★

Les Dawson, the British comedian, said: 'I'm feeling very lonely. I've been married for 15 years and yesterday my wife ran off with the chap next door. I'm going to miss him terribly.'

★ ☆ ★

On the death of her husband, his widow was inconsolable. She wept for three days inconsolably. When the insurance company's agent turned up with a cheque for £50,000 on her husband's life policy, her tears dried up. 'You won't believe it,' she said to the agent, 'but I would give £20,000 of this to have him back.'

• News Report, 1981

★ ☆ ★

To the man in the street, who, I'm sorry to say
Is a key observer of life
The word 'intellectual' suggests straight away
A man who's untrue to his wife.

• W H Auden

★ ☆ ★

To me passionate love has always been like a tight shoe rubbing blisters on my achilles heel.

• Noël Coward, quoted by Giles Brandreth, *Sunday Telegraph*, 21.11.99

★ ☆ ★

Chip shop owner Geoff Rhodes called in a pilot when he wanted to tell the world how he felt about his wife, Pauline, after two years' marriage.

But the plane towing a 'Happy Anniversary' message over their home in Meopham, Kent, yesterday was three hours late because of fog: the word 'anniversary' and Geoff's name were spelled wrongly, and it dropped the banner after ten minutes.

Finally, the pilot had to crash-land in a rugby field after narrowly missing a bus, causing £8,000 damage to his aircraft. But Mrs Rhodes said: 'It was the most romantic thing that has ever happened to me.'

• *Daily Mail*, 20.11.84

★ ☆ ★

John Bayley, widower of Dame Iris Murdoch, on the secret of marriage: 'Both participants have to be equally untidy and want to go to bed at the same time.'

• Jasper Gerard, *The Times*, 26.3.99

★ ☆ ★

When the Italian Ambassador was having lunch with the British Defence Minister, John Nott, he congratulated Mr Nott on being 50 years old that very day. 'Fifty is a marvellous age,' said the Italian Ambassador. 'When a woman says "yes" you are flattered and when she says "no" you are relieved.'

★ ☆ ★

I never rated a man enough to give his diamonds back.

• Zsa Zsa Gabor

★ ☆ ★

Those who reached puberty in 1960 or later aren't exactly teenagers now, but an awful lot of people still seem to think that until about the time of the Pill, the Beatles and the Lady Chatterley trial everyone was a virgin on their wedding night, mated for life like swallows and would be ordered out into the cold, cold snow by their fathers if they confessed to being pregnant.

• Katherine Whitehorn, *Guardian*, 22.10.98

★ ☆ ★

Maurice Chevalier, the French singer and actor, was asked why he had chosen to remain a bachelor. 'You're not going to believe this,' he replied, 'but it's for a very good reason. When I get up in the morning, I like to have the choice of getting out of bed from either side.'

• *Faber Book of Anecdotes*, edited by Clifton Fadiman

23 Millenniums Take Time

modern living, manners and the millennium

A librarian from Ely, Cambridgeshire, has won a computer for answering this year's most obscure request for information from a member of the public – how to build a Mongolian yurt.

• Society, *Guardian*, 10.11.99

★ ☆ ★

A piece of fossilised woolly mammoth dung and an 18th-century ivory sex toy are among the stranger purchases people have made over the Internet, according to a new poll. The most popular online sales are CDs, books, and train and concert tickets but shoppers are also using the Web to buy more obscure items. Internet retailer Egg Shop polled 4,000 customers to find out the most unusual items they had purchased. At the top of the list was a Mongolian beard-crimper, real estate on the Moon, live maggots, a stuffed giraffe, liquid latex body-paint and smoked boar meat. The poll also found shoppers were taking advantage of the privacy the Internet affords to buy underwear, sex toys and contraception. Almost a third of orders placed through the Egg Shop pharmacy retailers were by men for condoms and hair treatment products.

• *Metro*, 20.6.00

★ ☆ ★

It Takes All Sorts

Here we are, the turn of the Millennium, and what I want to know is, what happened to the flying cars? People have been predicting what we'd be like for more than 1000 years, and our accoutrements don't entirely live up to expectations. No airborne automobiles. No space-liners to extraterrestrial vacation spots – we can't even deliver that mechanical thing to Mars in working order. No house-cleaning robots. No moving sidewalks, except those deeply unsatisfactory ones in airports. One of the reasons the popular prognosticators of the past never got us right is because they tended to envision our lives as filled with the same things they already had, only better. They didn't conceive of computers or faxes; they thought about pneumatic tubes going really, really fast. They predicted something approaching radio. But they never figured out television, possibly because they couldn't stretch their minds around what having a perpetual entertainment machine in every living room would do to family life. So we march into the Millennium, gravity-bound, traffic-clogged and roach-infested as ever, less efficient, but maybe more human, than anybody anticipated.

• Adam Marks, *New York Times*. 31.12.99

★ ☆ ★

Technology hasn't failed us; we have failed technology. We can't think of anything of consequence to do with it. And since there's only going to be technology from now on, it's night-night to the grown-ups. Welcome to the most infantile century in the history of mankind, and take a last look at what I'm addressing you with – they're called *words*.

Yet for all that, I'm pleased to have got here. Never mind what I am going to find in 2000, is it not a miracle of continuance that I am here to find anything? Foolish, I know, given that millions of people older and more infirm than I am (and there's one cheery thought, at least) have also made it through. But they've probably done it with deliberation. Steered their course. Kept an eye on their progress. Whereas I am around only by some species of unconscious endurance.

What happens when you endure, so to speak by accident, is that you become liable to over-exaggerate your own remarkableness. By God, the heart still pumps, the bladder still fills and empties, the toes still curl, I am a prodigy! I sometimes wonder whether I might not have inherited the most extraordinary genes, so remorseless seems to be my protraction. Don't get me wrong – this is not vanity. Quite the opposite. For it is not by virtue of anything I have done that I persevere. It is fluke. I have fluked my genes, and no man can be vain about what is given him by chance. What is more, I now see only too clearly how my apparent good fortune will make a fool of me.

• Howard Jacobson, *Independent*. 2.1.00

★ ☆ ★

The Millennium Dome seems to me the outstandingly funny idea of the past decade, and the joke seems to grow funnier with each fresh pronouncement by Peter Mandelson. But now, when I read Bel Littlejohn's *Millennium Dome Diary*, I find it hard to separate my cheap made-up jokes from the minister's real multi-million-pound ones. It is almost as if he was working to my blueprint. Is it really called the New Millennium Dome Experience? Is Rupert Murdoch really sponsoring a zone? Is its slogan really 'Time to Make a Difference?' Is a virtual-reality Archbishop of Canterbury really to be transported around the Spirit Zone on a cloud at speeds of up to 350 mph?

One final blow. For years, my fellow humorists and I have been struggling to crack jokes about mobile phones. This week, I read a true story of a man in Brazil who stepped out of a shower, skidded on the floor and ended up with a mobile phone jammed up his bottom. The phone rang three times before hospital staff managed to remove it. With the world already so comical, is it any wonder so many humorists are queuing for stress-counselling?

• Craig Brown, *Daily Telegraph*, 24.10.98

⋆ ☆ ⋆

I have been reading an article in the *Express* about the 'hotel of the future'. It is a hotel in which 'as you step in the lift, it purrs out your name, wishes you a nice stay and points out that the first drink is on the house.' Then, when you get into your room, the television set takes up this one-sided conversation. It tells you that your favourite drink is chilling in the mini-bar and that the room temperature has been set at the level you prefer. It then tells you that it has drawn up a list of TV programmes that it thinks you might enjoy, and adds that if you are feeling like going out that evening, it can obtain cheap theatre tickets for you and order you a taxi.

Somehow – though the article doesn't explain how – the hotel's computer knows all about you in advance: your hopes, your fears, your secret yearnings. A 'data analysis expert' called Alistair Sim – a kinsman of the great Scottish actor, perhaps? – is quoted by the *Express* as saying: 'By collecting as much information about an individual as possible, not only can likes and dislikes be stored and analysed; the whole "historical" record of a person can be stored and compared to group norms to discover behavioural likelihood.'

One is obviously worried about the methods that hotels plan to use for discovering one's 'behavioural likelihood'. But more alarming still is the prospect in the future of having to conduct more and more conversations with disembodied voices. For computers are already able to listen as well as talk. My wife has a telephone answering service that asks her questions, to which she must reply yes or no (though it often fails to understand her answers). In the future, such conversations will be far more sophisticated and elaborate.

• Alexander Chancellor, *Guardian*, 23.1.99

★ ☆ ★

Never eat at a place called Mom's, as the old American homily tells us, never play poker with a guy called Doc and never lie down with a woman who has more problems than you do. To these home-spun precepts may I now add a fourth: never leap from your bath to take a call from New York. You may regret it.

Programmed after years on *The Sunday Times Magazine* to believe any call from the Big Apple was likely to be important or at least interesting – a writer or photographer with a good idea, for instance – I emerged from a hot tub last week to take such a call, only to find myself listening to a smooth-talking young Yank who was keen to sell me shares; or as they would say, stock.

Only a few days before that I had been called by a young hopeful from Hilversum anxious to sell me Spanish lottery tickets. God knows where the horror will strike from next. With the collapse of communism, there could soon be salesmen calling from St Petersburg to sell you life assurance or from Dubrovnik to talk you into double glazing.

• Godfrey Smith, *The Sunday Times*, 21.1.96

★ ☆ ★

There comes a time when being politically correct means being idiotically wrong. And never more so than when the good burghers of Redditch decided that allowing performers in an amateur production of *Show Boat* to black their faces was contrary to good race relations.

They know nothing about the theatre and its history. They know nothing about blackface. And they know even less about good race relations.

What they need to know is that *Show Boat* was an incredibly brave venture. When it opened in New York in 1927 – the same year, incidentally, that a blacked-up Al Jolson appeared in the world's first talking picture, *The Jazz Singer* – it defied every statute in the black-white canon. 'Coloured' workers – a term that black Americans themselves used when they set up the still extant National Association for the Advancement of Colored People – were shown to be labouring under the whip of oppression.

The opening lines of the show's big number, Ol' Man River, stated that 'Niggers all work on the Mississippi'. Paul Robeson, the greatest of all black artists, sang that. No one wants to say it at Redditch. But those words, like the black faces of the singers, were vital to the intentions of the lyricist, Oscar Hammerstein II.

As his son, Oscar Hammerstein III, told me: 'It was the most perfect demonstration of just how hard the labours of the black river workers really were. It shocked even then.' But the message got across. In that terrible word, sung by a black man, centuries of slavery were conveyed as surely as the sweat pouring off the backs of the men hauling the cotton on to the river boats. A white man who didn't black his face could never sing that song.

The councillors who have put their collective foot down – in their mouth as much as on the floor of the council chamber – also need to know something about the history of blackface. It was a theatrical convention used at a time when black actors and actresses were virtually banned from the stages of both Britain and America. It was such an accepted convention that when the great 'coloured' vaudevillian Bert Williams appeared in the world-famous Ziegfeld Follies, even he blacked up – because the producer thought Williams' skin was too light.

Did he take offence? For him, it was an opportunity to present black culture to audiences who had never seen a member of his race on the stage before – or only as a slobbering, stupid manservant or a black mammy, both of whom laughed and bowed and scraped at the 'masser's' command.

• Michael Freedland, *Guardian*, 27.8.99

★ ☆ ★

Even if nobody else is very impressed with British Technology, the technologists continue to ensure that our own dear Royal Family are, and at any cost. When the Queen Mother was opening the new Ministry of Pensions Computer Centre in Newcastle some time ago she was invited to press a button, and the great machine immediately leapt into pulsating life, churning out long strips of paper printed with the correct answers to questions previously fed into it by the bland demonstrator.

But what the Queen Mother was not told was that the answers had in fact been printed the night before in case anything went wrong on the big day, and that there was at that moment a man crouched down behind the amazing machinery feeding them through by hand.

A similar situation arose when Her Majesty the Queen was asked to initiate the infallible STD service from Bristol. Standing at her elbow, the beaming Postmaster General explained that she had only to lift the receiver, dial the number he told her, and she would be able to speak to the Lord Provost of Glasgow. Explaining with an endearing modesty that she hadn't much of a head for numbers, Her Majesty asked what would happen if she made a mistake in dialling. The PMG's face dropped slightly as he leant forward and breathed, 'Actually, Your Majesty, it doesn't matter what number you dial, you will still get the Lord Provost of Glasgow.'

• *Private Eye* 4.2.66

★ ☆ ★

It Takes All Sorts

Life is extinct on other planets because their scientists were more advanced than ours.

• John F Kennedy

★ ☆ ★

It's easy to tell when you've got a bargain. It doesn't fit.

• Anon

★ ☆ ★

People, like me, who have lived for many years in a big city have been so long accustomed to indifference, or even rudeness, on the part of our fellow citizens that we have to come to be quite appreciative of it.

It may not be pleasant when a person for whom you have opened a door fails to thank you for doing so, or when somebody who has shoved you roughly off the pavement and into the street doesn't even acknowledge your pathetic apology for having been in his way. But you soon learn not to open doors for people and not to apologise to them, especially for things that are entirely their fault. Once you have learned not to thank and not to apologise, you feel not only less offended when others don't thank or apologise to you, but you feel an altogether more relaxed person. The constant anxiety about trying to please goes. The strain on the facial muscles disappears. You can just go around being a cool bastard like everybody else.

If there is one thing that all great cities, apart from London, have in common, it is that they pride themselves on their bad manners. The people of New York, Paris and Rome are all the same. They actively delight in a reputation for bloody-mindedness, they enjoy being unhelpful to tourists, and they cherish the conceit that only they have the guts and the cleverness to meet the tough, everyday challenges of city life.

But London is a bit different. It has a lot of bloody-mindedness, particularly among certain groups, such as taxi-drivers, but most citizens are embarrassed about it. They are pleased and grateful when foreigners say how 'civilised' London is. They want to be thought of as warm, neighbourly and caring. But they don't want to be thought of as cool or sophisticated.

• Alexander Chancellor, *Guardian*, 16.1.99

★ ☆ ★

When the Royal Family travel, the whole question of their lavatories is an exercise in the balance of the sacred with the profane. 'Her, in there?' It is a widespread belief in Britain that new, pristine lavatories are required for royal visits. Anecdotes abound. At Girton College, Cambridge, they say a lavatory was renovated and then closed to all for two full months before a visit from the Queen Mother. And that St Mary Abbot's Hospital in Kensington installed a special pink seat for Princess Margaret's short visit and she did not even use it. The Tate Gallery in London solves the problem by having what the staff call 'the Royal loo', a permanent fixture used only on royal occasions. The *Daily Mirror* has run articles about special facilities built on station platforms or factory floors and then dismantled after the royal visit without anyone else getting a chance to use them. (Who is being protected against whom? Freud might ask.)

To all these stories, Buckingham Palace replies, 'Absolute piffle!' The Queen never asks for special arrangements, the Palace says. What happens is that royal visits are often used as an occasion, or even an excuse, for modernising the lavatory, buying new carpet, painting the walls. Added to that is the overwhelming feeling of anyone receiving the Queen that everything must be at the best it possibly can be, and so they renovate. Then word of the decorating gets out and it is assumed that the Queen has demanded it. 'People get it exactly the wrong way round,' a spokesman said.

• Brenda Maddox, *Guardian*, 14.11.73

★ ☆ ★

That's the great thing about after-dinner speaking – you get the room and you get spoilt rotten. If you were the cabaret and you arrived at a hotel, and you said, 'Is there anywhere I can change?' they'd say: 'The gents is down the corridor.' If you're the after-dinner speaker, they say: 'Do you want to come to the penthouse and meet Sir Charles, the chairman?' You're the same idiot, but you get treated totally different.

• Barry Cryer, interviewed by Richard Johnson, *The Sunday Times Magazine*, 21.3.99

★ ☆ ★

Sir Richard Branson's efficiency objectives seem to have created a trap for rail users with old-fashioned ideas about courtesy. Yesterday, I accompanied my octogenarian mother-in-law to Birmingham International station to put her on the train home to Manchester, where she was to be met by a niece.

There were no porters around, of course, so I helped the old lady up the train steps – she is a little stiff in the joints these days – guided her to her reserved seat and placed her suitcase in the rack. I suppose it took half a minute at most. I then made to hop off the train to wave her goodbye.

Only then did I discover that the train doors were locked. I lowered the window and asked the guard, who was nearby, if he could please let me off as I wasn't going anywhere. 'You are now, sir,' he said cheerfully, and explained that the driver now electronically locks the doors 30 seconds before moving off. They would not open again until the next station, he added.

Fortunately, it was not a non-stop service to Manchester, and my enforced journey was only eight miles up the line to

Birmingham New Street. The incident caused some merriment back home.

But I have learnt the hard way that in future I am expected to push the old lady unceremoniously up the train steps, throw her suitcase in after her and leave her to fend for herself.

• Maurice Weaver, Solihull, W. Midlands, letter to the *Daily Telegraph*, 29.10.98

⋆ ☆ ⋆

Christmas presents should always be shiny. The most discerning person will often mistake shininess for expensiveness.

• P G Wodehouse

⋆ ☆ ⋆

I dislike arguments of any kind. They are always vulgar and often convincing.

• Oscar Wilde

⋆ ☆ ⋆

To stop an argument in its tracks when someone is claiming that the average wage is £70 in England or that the divorce rate is 30% in Italy or violence has risen by 15% in America, you can always intervene with the discussion-stopping remark 'But not in the south.'

• Stephen Potter

⋆ ☆ ⋆

I thought that every man must know that a *short* jacket is always worn with a silk hat at a private view in the morning.

• King Edward VII

24 What Makes Them Different?

people

Apology of the year: Runner-up, the *Daily Star*: 'The Pope. We reported on April 9 that Pope John Paul II supported Fulham. We have been asked to point out that, although the Vatican may have written to the club, the Pope is not a Fulham man.'

• Captain Moonlight, *Independent* 26.12.99

★ ☆ ★

Africa's weirdest explorer, the indomitable Gordon Laing, crossed the Sahara in search of the Niger and the mythical Eldorado of Timbuctoo. After 400 miles strapped onto the back of a camel, he emerged from the desert with plentiful sabre cuts, a fractured jawbone, a musket ball in the hip, three broken fingers and a slashed wrist, and suffering from a yellow fever-like plague.

'I am nevertheless doing well,' he confided Pythonesquely in his journal, 'and hope yet to return to England with much important geographical information.'

'Laing was mad,' says Fleming. 'But a lot of slightly mad people are very plausible.' The withered, limping Laing entered Timbuctoo in August 1826, the first white man ever to do so only to discover a sordid, mud-brick town instead of the palaces of gold he had expected. He was murdered within a month.

• Peter Aspden, reviewing *Barrow Boys* by Fergus Fleming. *Financial Times*, 24.10.98

★ ☆ ★

After 20 minutes waiting for a train on the Docklands Light Railway yesterday, one passenger confronted an official. When the official seemed surprised at the accusation, the passenger pointed at the people standing four-deep on the platform and asked: 'If there hasn't been a delay, why are all those passengers still there?' To which the official replied: 'They are not passengers, they are tourists.'

Meanwhile, I wonder what passengers are called in South Africa. *Railway Gazette International* reports the results of a campaign against on-train crime. 'Improved door locks and hopper windows prevent thugs from throwing passengers from the train.'

• Diary, *Independent*.

★ ☆ ★

The real accusation against Terence Conran, the indefensible blemish we can't forgive him, is his smugness. He is one of those self-proclaimed gurus like Peter York who had their heydey in the eighties, who believe appearance and design is all, and just how boring is that?

Ask Conran which design he most admires and he smugly says 'the paperclip', which he deems 'really quite brilliant' and 'a very good example of how we take design for granted'.

There's more design drivel when he gets on to the milk bottle. 'Milk bottles have disappeared from my life and I miss them.' He speaks of them as one might speak of the dearly departed. 'They were pleasant to hold and good-looking – I was always happy to put one on the table.'

• Gabrielle Morris, *Guardian* Review, 7.11.98

★ ☆ ★

The 8th Earl of Clancarty, who died in 1995 aged 83, was an absolute gift to the comic obituarist. He devoted his life to propagating belief in flying saucers:

Brinsley Clancarty, a tall, amiable figure with a rather haunted expression and elegant braces, claimed that he could trace his descent from 63,000 BC, when beings from other planets had landed on Earth in space-ships. Most humans, he said, were descended from these aliens: 'This accounts for all the different colour skins we've got here,' he said in 1981.

A few of these early aliens did not come from space, he explained, but emerged through tunnels from a civilisation which still existed beneath the Earth's crust. There were seven or eight of these tunnels altogether, one at the North Pole, another at the South Pole, and others in such places as Tibet. 'I haven't been down there myself,' Clancarty said, 'but from what I gather [these beings] are very advanced.'

• Bevis Hillier, *Spectator*, 4.12.99, reviewing *The Daily Telegraph Fifth Book of Obituaries*, ed. Hugh Massingberd

★ ☆ ★

I knew I was being unreasonable because of feeling low – but still, the New York art world is pretty hard to take at the best of times. About a month ago, I went to a party in another Soho loft. This place was cluttered with racks of Mills and Boon paperbacks and giant plastic potted plants like you get in airports, and wall-unit displays of porno magazines. It turned out that the hostess of this soirée, a red-haired woman in her early twenties, called Pagan or Axel or something, was an artist and all this horrible stuff was her work. Oh. Oh, how interesting.

Boy, did I take a dislike to Pagan. She had an old factory time-clock up on the wall in her hallway, together with all the old punch cards of the people who used to work at the factory. This was another of her artworks – a witty tribute to the fascinating (and, let's face it, rather sexy) world of blue-collar labour. Pagan really did make you nostalgic for the days of compulsory national service.

Anyway, to get back to this week's dinner: the host insisted on playing loud rock music. At one point, he asked me to put another record on. At the bottom of his pile of nasty rock CDs, I found a nice old Harry Belafonte tape. Everyone was outraged. It was 'black music for white people' someone said, and all the other guests nodded sagely. I said I thought that (a) Harry Belafonte would be surprised to hear that and (b) it if was black music for white people, then it was altogether fitting, since everyone present was white. This line of argument did not go down well, and halfway through 'Island in the Sun', the tape was rudely pulled out.

Then the host decided that he wanted to dance. Everyone in turn had to get up and cavort about the room with him to Prince's 'The Most Beautiful Girl in the World' (which apparently counts as black music for black people). I decided it was time to leave. The host felt that I owed him a long public goodbye snog. I did not. There was an unseemly tussle which everyone at the dinner table watched with a sort of silent, zombie fascination. After I had successfully fought him and his tongue off, my host turned nasty and said my new haircut made me look like an Avon lady. I smiled very sweetly and bade the company goodbye.

• Zoe Heller, *Independent on Sunday*, 21.8.94

★ ☆ ★

Sir, Recent references to Field Marshal Montgomery have reminded me of an experience when I was teaching in the early 1960s.

I took a party of boys to visit Westminster Abbey and the Houses of Parliament. When we were walking along Whitehall I spotted Monty leaving a saloon car and walking towards the War Office. I called to my pupils to run with me towards him.

We arrived in time at the entrance and I stood to attention, saluted and stated my rank, name and number. He looked at each boy and pointing a finger he uttered: 'Haircut; haircut; haircut.'

• Ralph Barnes, letter to *The Times*, 28.1.99

* ☆ *

One of the most touching experiences last week offered was the British mathematician Andrew Wiles dissolving in tears on BBC TV's *Horizon* programme as he described the moment he finally cracked Fermat's Last Theorem. It's a problem that has baffled mathematicians for 300 years and took him seven years locked in his loft to solve. The solution, he confided to us, had proved 'so indescribably beautiful, so simple and so elegant.'

He was by no means the first mathematician to feel like that. 'Beauty is the first test,' wrote G H Hardy in his marvellous little book *A Mathematician's Apology*. 'There is no place in the world for ugly mathematics.' Yet maths, to the layman, seems sometimes to hover perilously on the verge of nonsense.

'Mathematics,' declared Bertrand Russell, 'may be defined as the subject in which we never know what we are talking about nor whether what we are saying is true.' Einstein concurred: 'As far as the laws of mathematics refer to reality, they are not certain, and as far as they are certain, they do not refer to reality.'

It's hardly surprising, then, if mathematicians sometimes give the impression of belonging to alternative worlds. As one Oxbridge college head put it to me: 'They do rather tend to sit staring into space.' What are they seeing?

• Godfrey Smith, *The Sunday Times*, 21.1.96

* ☆ *

Invitations – in the name of 'the Committee for the Celebration of Bruce Bernard's outstanding weaknesses' – have gone out to a wake for the Soho veteran. Bernard specified before his death how he'd like to be seen off: 'Plenty of good things to eat and drink must be served. If I were there, I would especially like cold lamb cooked to a dull pink throughout – also the best rare beef. Potato salad made with the finest potatoes and dressing would seem imperative. I may well, it will be appreciated, never see another potato again, and Branston Pickle seems to me a very good thing. Please excuse this disgusting paragraph. Absolutely no one should be barred unless determined to make themselves really obnoxious. All this is VANITY and VEXATION OF SPIRIT, but enjoyably so, I would hope.'

• Peterborough, *Daily Telegraph*, 4.5.00

★ ☆ ★

When the famous conductor, Sir Malcolm Sargent, was visited at his home by a close friend, he was introduced to a tall, distinguished man who rose from his chair in the living room.

'His Royal Highness, the King of Norway,' said Sargent. To which the tall man, inclining his head and stretching out his hand, muttered, 'Sweden.'

★ ☆ ★

A man in Shropshire while playing billiards in a pub accidentally knocked the cue chalk into one of the pockets. As he leaned over to take out the chalk he coughed and his false teeth flew into the pocket. Reaching down to recover his teeth, his hand got stuck in the ribbed pocket and he couldn't get it out. Some 50 customers crowded round offering such advice as soaking his arm in washing up liquid, all to no avail. Finally they had to call in two policemen and six firemen to take the billiard table apart before the victim could be freed and the game resume with his false teeth where they ought to be in his mouth.

• News Report, 1979

★ ☆ ★

Late in the 1920s the writer H G Wells helped to finance a peace ship to be sailed from Britain to America to proclaim the virtues of peace. Needing influential financial support, he arranged an interview with Herbert Hoover in the White House to expound the importance of his idea. The American President listened for a half hour to the great novelist as he passionately expounded his idea. Then Hoover, indicating that the appointment was over, looked at his watch and said, 'Thank you very much for what you have told me. I would like to hear more but I must now meet my next visitor, who is waiting to see me outside, the famous English novelist, Mr H G Wells.'

★ ☆ ★

Diana Vreeland in her autobiography tells of going to see a film called *L'Atlantide* in Paris in the 1920s. It was very hot and the only seats available were in the third balcony. The film was about Foreign Legion soldiers in the desert who find an oasis occupied by a beautiful woman on a throne surrounded by cheetahs! When one of the soldiers approaches her, she gives him a glass of champagne and he drinks it. She takes the glass from him, breaks it, and cuts his throat with it.

Miss Vreeland was spellbound by the curious mood of the film, by this queen of a Lost Continent and her cheetahs. Then the lights went on and she felt a slight movement under her hand. She looked down – and it was a cheetah! And beside the cheetah was Josephine Baker, the black cabaret artiste who was admired by all Paris.

'Oh,' said Diana Vreeland, 'you've brought your cheetah to see the cheetahs.'

'Yes,' said Josephine Baker, 'that's exactly what I did.'

She was alone with the cheetah on a lead. She was wearing a shirt with no sleeves, no back, no front – just crossed bars on a bias.

Getting out of the cinema, the cheetah dragged those long black legs down three flights of stairs at a terrific speed. Outside there was an enormous white and silver Rolls Royce waiting for her. The cheetah whooped and took one leap into the back of the Rolls and they were off. That was speed and style.

• Diana Vreeland in her Autobiography.

★ ☆ ★

When I am making a speech I do not worry overmuch if members of the audience start looking at their watches, but if they start shaking them to see if the watch has stopped, I get concerned.

• Lord Birkett

★ ☆ ★

H G Wells was a cad who didn't pretend to be anything but a cad. Arnold Bennett was a cad pretending to be a gentleman. Bernard Shaw was a gentleman pretending to be a cad.

• Hilaire Belloc

★ ☆ ★

Florence Nightingale was a hypochondriac who took to her bed after the Crimean War in 1857 convinced that she had terminal heart disease. She remained bedridden, always claiming that her life hung by a thread, until she died 54 years later in 1910 at the age of 90.

★ ☆ ★

You may think, as I say, that a man's choice of hairdresser is of little moment, and that, provided they do not cut their clients' ears off or apply a powerfully corrosive acid instead of lotion, anyone is as good as any other. You would be profoundly mistaken, but hairdressers differ as heads differ, and as the characters beneath those heads, too, and the true master of the art matches not only his tonsorial style, but his chairside manner, to the man on whom he is operating; from the first I knew that Mr East was the scissorer for me.

Take the question of talking. King Archilaus of Macedon (*floruit* 400 BC) touched on this very point when, in response to his barber's question, 'How would you like your hair cut, Sire?' replied 'In silence' (this, incidentally, making the earliest recorded joke in human history).

Thus, most impeccably, it has always been with Mr East; he may offer a word of two about the political situation (couched in non-partisan terms), an anecdote or incident, something of his family (this year marks his ruby wedding as well as his retirement, and a forthcoming grandchild, too), his garden or his holiday, but he never goes on unless it is clear I want to, and more often than not I sink into a semi-hypnotized silence, and allow the regular snip of the scissors to provide a soothing and peaceful atmosphere in which (I always make the appointment for the early morning) to start the day.

I have never learned from Mr East how he decided on the calling he has followed for so many years, nor how he acquired such skill in it, though I have gathered that he took it up on returning from the war. No doubt such skill can be achieved by years of hard work, though some gift for it is surely also necessary. But be that as it may, Mr East is one of those who keep the world spinning in its proper orbit by maintaining the essential character of *homo faber*; to cut hair skilfully is not so great a contribution to civilization as to write the *Jupiter Symphony*, but it is a contribution none the less. Not because it is of great importance that hair should be cut well, for we could all get along without much difficulty if we all looked like frights on emerging from the hairdresser's: but because it is of great, indeed of crucial importance that there should continue to be men and women who scorn to take their wages for a job ill done, and would do their job well even if there was no one about to see.

• Bernard Levin, *The Times*, 1977

★ ☆ ★

Winston Churchill spent the best years of his life preparing his impromptu speeches.

★ ☆ ★

Stephen Spender, a popular poet in the 1930s, had a reputation for being muddle-headed when all around him had made up their minds about their political orientations. When he finally pledged his services to the Republicans in the Spanish Civil War, he was told by Harry Pollit, an old-time communist, 'Go and get killed, comrade, we need a Byron in the Movement.'

★ ☆ ★

Catherine Griffiths, who died in 1968 at the age of 102, had a reputation as a radical and prominent suffragette. Her finest moment perhaps was when she stole into the chamber of the House of Commons and strewed tin tacks upon the seat of the British Prime Minister, Lloyd George. It was 'to make him sit up,' she later explained.

• *Daily Telegraph Book of Obituaries of Eccentric Lives*, edited by Hugh Massingberd

★ ☆ ★

It is just not true that the world wants to know about Mr Clinton's sex life out of concern for the efficacy of the presidency. It's an *excuse*, dammit! Not true that news of Robin Cook's philandering is awaited with an impatience born of anxiety for the dignity of Britain's foreign policy. Snakes alive, the reason's clear as daylight. The public is inquisitive. We gossip, we pry, we tut-tut and we giggle. We love scandal, we love drama, we love a human story. Mankind has always thrilled most readily to a tale of the loves and hates, sins and hopes, secrets and fears, of other men and women.

It hardly matters if the cast is real or fictional. The urge is to know what happens to characters in *Eastenders, Pride and Prejudice, The Archers* or the latest Jilly Cooper bonkbuster. It is the same urge as drives our fascination with indiscretion in the Oval Office, or the pillows on which Mr Cook may have laid his gingery beard. Media excitement about the shape of Mr Clinton's penis is in no wise different from the recent Internet frenzy to see rogue pictures of Leonardo DiCaprio in the nude. It is fatuous to pretend that concern for the public interest is what motivates curiosity about politicians' private lives. It's the other way round: human curiosity drives the search for a 'public interest' justification for such stories.

• Matthew Parris, *The Times*, 9.1.99

★ ☆ ★

Sir George Everett meticulously made the calculation in the 19th century that Mount Everest was precisely 29,000 feet. When he revealed his figures, he added two feet to its height to 29,002 feet because he felt that people would be suspicious of a nice round figure of 29,000 and that 29,002 feet would give it an aura of scientific responsibility.

★ ☆ ★

IT TAKES ALL SORTS

Einstein having hit upon his relativity equation $E=mc^2$, came downstairs in his nightshirt and bedroom slippers and said to his wife, 'Mamma, I have a little new idea.'

★ ☆ ★

When Johann Strauss, the Waltz King, fell ill, his brother Josef (an architect) felt compelled to keep the family tradition going. So he wrote a waltz which he firmly titled 'The First and Last'. It was a brilliant success, so he wrote another which he described as 'The First *After* the Last'. Then he wrote 250 more.

• Richard Morrison, *The Times*, 28.1.00

★ ☆ ★

The survival of bookmakers is a matter of deep concern to me and I spend sleepless nights worrying about them. I give them whatever I can, but I'm afraid it isn't enough. You see, I love bookmakers. I love the way they shout and I love the way they smile when they see me coming. I love the way they buy me tea on the race train and I love the way they offer me credit.

The world is full of idiots like me who will bet on anything and for the life of me I can't understand why bookmakers aren't catering for us. It isn't enough to lay horses, dogs, political parties and football teams, oh no. I want to see nearly everything and everyone laid. Every day I look for 100-8 that a London taxi driver will be polite to me. And why can't I get 10-1 that the next 10 women I talk to will tell me to go away in two words consisting of no more than seven letters? I also want to bet on how many more bets I've got to strike before I make a winning one.

• Jeffrey Bernard, quoted by David Ashforth, *Racing Post*, 26.8.99

★ ☆ ★

In 1946 Joe Louis, world heavyweight champion, was preparing to defend his title against Billy Conn for the second time. He was warned to watch out for Conn's great speed and his tactic of darting in to the attack and then moving speedily out of his opponent's range. Replying to this professional but useless advice, Louis replied confidently, 'He can run, but he can't hide.'

• *Faber Book of Anecdotes*, edited by Clifton Fadiman.

Joe Louis

25 Politics Is A Blood Sport

politics and politicians

When Karl Marx suggested that capitalism would create its own gravediggers it seems unlikely that he had in mind a motley collection of individuals dressed as turtles and butterflies, jigging around with giant inflatable dolphins to the beat of native drums, whose slogans ranged from 'Barbie Kills' and 'Trust Jesus' to 'Free Tibet' and 'Go Vegan' and whose aims were apparently endorsed by the President of the United States. The 'demonstration against capitalism' in Seattle and its runt offspring in London, staged during the World Trade Organisation conference, captured well the degraded state of radical politics at the century's end.

Protest organisers claim that the wide range of issues raised shows their movement's strength. In fact, those who protest against everything end up challenging nothing in particular. The disparate demonstrations against capitalism represented more of a general moan about life than a movement to change the world.

For many of the protesters this kind of gesture politics is primarily an exercise in self-flattery. Those who claim to speak for the masses often end up expressing a kind of exclusive moral elitism. Their message is that 'I am a better person than you', because they don't eat at McDonald's, or buy clothes from stores with politically incorrect names such as Banana Republic, and they were once pushed by a policeman.

If this is what anti-capitalism has become it poses less of a threat to the powers that be than at any time over the past two centuries. For all their talk about protecting the world's poor, many of the *fin de siècle* anti-capitalists' proposed measures of environmental protectionism would hit Third World economies hardest.

• Mick Hume, *The Times* 6.12.99

★ ☆ ★

For those who feel the passion's gone from politics, here's a tale from Tennessee. Tommy Burks, the popular Democrat incumbent in the state Senate race, has just been shot dead on his pig farm. This leaves only his unpopular Republican challenger, Byron Low Tax Looper, on the ballot paper. One small problem: Looper, described by friends as paranoid, has just been arrested for murdering Burks but, because he won't be convicted before polling day, he looks likely to be elected anyway. Is this what Blair's thinking of when he champions more robust local politics and elected mayors?

• Andrew Marr, *Daily Express*, 28.10.98

★ ☆ ★

When they set out to change the world, most protesters are dismissed as nuisances, cranks or dangerous threats to the status quo. Some were considered so dangerous that they were assassinated (Gandhi, Trotsky, Kennedy, Martin Luther King). Some were imprisoned (Mandela, Vaclav Havel). Solzhenitsyn was exiled, Steve Biko beaten to death. Even in Stalin's gulags, men and women made their mental notes for posterity.

'For years,' Martin Luther King wrote from Birmingham Jail, 'I have heard the word "wait". It rings in the ear of every negro with piercing familiarity. This "wait" has almost always meant "never". It is the men and women who refuse to believe in "never" who change the human lot – and who lit the candle for those who protest today.'

• Brian MacArthur, *Independent*, 21.10.98

★ ☆ ★

As political scandals go it is hardly up there with 'cash for questions', 'arms to Iraq' or the Profumo affair; but the Tories in Wales are none the less getting mighty exercised about cheese sandwiches.

Claims of 'cheese sleaze' have been made after it emerged that Plaid Cymru offered voters a cup of tea and a sandwich at an agricultural show, just days before a local council by-election.

Peter Davies, the chairman of South East Wales Conservatives, said the Plaid Cymru candidate, Darren Jones, was guilty of a 'very serious breach of election law. If it had just been a cup of tea or coffee we probably wouldn't have done anything but when it comes to sandwiches it is the thin end of the wedge.'

Mrs English, who sparked the controversy, added: 'The sandwiches were very nice but they didn't influence my vote. If the Tories had been offering chocolate cake I would have eaten it but I still wouldn't have voted for them.'

• Kate Watson-Smyth, *Independent*, 29.8.98

★ ☆ ★

In the last decade of the 19th century, the headmasters of Eton and Winchester wrote to the Home Office to complain about the amount of pornography their pupils were obtaining from abroad. The Home Secretary, anxious to protect the moral integrity of the ruling class, issued a series of warrants authorising the Post Office to intercept suspected packages. Soon the Post Office complained that not only was its surveillance system being stretched to the limit, but that it did not want the legal responsibility of spying on people's mail because 'public sentiment is very strong in support of the supposed inviolability of letters passing through the post.'

This caused the government to consider passing a law authorising the Post Office's actions, but it backed away when its law officers advised that debate about such a law might well raise questions about the extent of the Home Secretary's powers under the recently passed Official Secrets Act (1889) – a highly undesirable state of affairs. As the author of this scholarly, timely and important book concludes, the case of the public schools and the pornographers is a microcosm of the problem that faces any government once it commits itself to legislation on secrecy – there is no going back.

So step by stealthy step, government after government found excuses to pass, amend and strengthen legislation protecting the manner in which the country was run, until today – as former Prime Minister Edward Heath has pointed out – Britain is the most secretive of all western democracies, and the habit of telling its citizens as little as possible has become ingrained in the ruling classes.

• Phillip Knightley, reviewing *The Culture of Secrecy in Britain in 1832–1996* by David Vincent

★ ☆ ★

Out meeting the public in his home town of Rotherham – always a risky business – William Hague, leader of the Conservative Party, knocked on a door and was met by an old woman who berated the Conservatives for not keeping their promises.

'How do you feel we let you down?' asked William. Came the reply: 'You never hanged the Kaiser.'

• Mandrake, *Sunday Telegraph*, 29.11.98

★ ☆ ★

Dr David Starkey has a scabrous take on Tony Blair's background: 'Jurisprudence has been the perfect preparation for his career: it is well-known to be a useless subject, full of high-sounding nothings, like his Third Way.'

• Diary, *The Times*, 9.11.98

★ ☆ ★

One of the many wonderful things we have learnt in the new political climate is that a little apology goes a long way, whoever you are. The Prime Minister has apologised to the Irish for the potato famine. Bill Clinton has travelled around Africa apologising for that whole unfortunate slavery thing. Paul Gascoigne, Will Carling and Teddy Sheringham have all been terribly contrite about some of the downright careless things they have done. In Australia, the government has even introduced a national Sorry Day, allowing craggy-faced Crocodile Dundee types to get in touch with their caring side by apologising gruffly to members of the indigenous population for certain inappropriate attitudes in the past: taking their land, calling them 'Abos', that kind of thing.

In this matter, at least, the politicians are in touch with the mood of the times. They realize that a few seconds of damp-eyed public emotion, however bogus, is worth hours of party political broadcasts. Who could be surprised that, following President Menem's apology last week – said to bear a striking resemblance to Emperor Akahito's semi-apology last year – there is now said to be an Apology Unit working in Downing Street to help public figures (presidents, emperors, even footballers) to present precisely the right kind of contrite public statement.

Presumably the Government's unit has developed an all-purpose statement which, with minor adaptations, can be used on any occasion, along the lines of: 'I, the President/the Emperor/the England striker; would like to express sincere regret for certain breaches of human rights/the war which took place between our countries /being found blotto at five in the morning in a lavatory with a bargirl. I hope to put the past behind me and, under the beneficent warmth of Britain's new, caring government, look forward to positive future relations with your country/your investors/my lovely wife and kids. Thanks very much, and now can I have those export credits/some nice tanks and aeroplanes/my place back in the England team?'

• Terence Blacker, *Independent*, 27.10.98

★ ☆ ★

Tony Benn's real-life diary entry for Sunday 26 December 1976 reads: 'Caroline gave each of us a copy of the *Communist Manifesto* in our stockings, published in English in Russia, and she gave Josh a book called *Marx for Beginners* and gave Hilary, Isaac Deutscher's three-volume biography of Trotsky.' This would have been far too unsubtle to publish as parody: one would have to think up something far less flat-footed than a stocking filled with the *Communist Manifesto* before anyone would even half believe it.

• Craig Brown, *Spectator*, 27.11.99

★ ☆ ★

To leave £4 million to a dog is the act of a supreme egotist. It's as near as can be got to leaving one's money to oneself, since it ensures that no other human being will enjoy it. The egotist in this case is the late Sidney Altman, of Los Angeles, whose will is being challenged by his ex-companion Marie Dana, who has an annual allowance for looking after the dog, but only until it dies.

In this country, another supreme egotist, Sir Edward Heath, is in the news because of an autobiography and an impending television profile. Sir Edward's egotism is legendary. I encountered it myself at the beginning of the 1970s when, as a reporter in Rome, I telephoned the Vatican to ask what gifts had been exchanged at a meeting between our then Prime Minister and the Pope. The Pope's gift had been facsimiles of the complete musical manuscripts of Palestrina from the Vatican archives, beautifully bound in leather; Sir Edward's had been a signed photograph of himself and a long-playing record of him conducting an orchestra.

Like Mr Altman, Sir Edward is both wifeless and childless; and, being 82, he may also by now have given thought to his will. Having no pet of his own, he may have been tempted to leave his considerable fortune to the ducks on the river at the bottom of his garden in Salisbury. Failing that, he has probably made generous provision for the care of his 1,100 boxes of personal papers. But as he sits there in his drawing-room, surrounded by photographs of himself with the giants of the 20th century, I hope he remembers his godchildren and also, of course, Dame Moura Lympany. She surely deserves a reward just for sparing him the agony of marriage.

• Alexander Chancellor, *Daily Telegraph*, 25.9.98

★ ☆ ★

As a rule, political 'what ifs' are distracting. As Mikhail Gorbachev reputedly said to a Western journalist who asked him what might have happened if Secretary Khruschev had been assassinated rather than President Kennedy, 'The rigorous analyst does not indulge in frivolous counter-factual speculation – but I don't think Mr Onassis would have married Mrs Khruschev.'

• Siôn Simon, *Daily Telegraph*, 10.4.00

★ ☆ ★

There is an unspoken premise (it is unspoken because if it were to be spoken it would at once collapse under the weight of its own absurdity) that politicians must be subject to more stringent rules of personal conduct than the rest of us because they are 'looked up to' and must therefore 'set an example'. Countless millions of would-be sinners, it seems, are held in check by the thought that if the Minister of State at the Department of the Environment and Local Government would never make a pass at the *au pair* it would ill become lesser mortals to do so, and that if, on the other hand, the Parliamentary Under-Secretary to the Ministry of Agriculture and Fisheries should in the absence of his wife be found in the attic, trouserless and not alone, it will signal to the nation that all standards have been abolished and the very beasts of the field are no longer safe from the effects of human depravity.

I am, as is well known, much given to hyperbole in the course of making a point with emphasis. I must therefore make clear that I am not employing this useful device when I say that in all my life I have never met any persons, in any trade or profession, whether educated or uneducated, sophisticated or naive, rich or poor, old, young or middle-aged, who would seek objective standards of moral behaviour, against which to measure their own, from our political leaders, or who would find otherwise than ridiculous or unintelligible the thought that they should.

See 'im in the 'ouse of Commons,
Passin' laws to put down crime,
While the girl that 'e 'as ruined
Picks 'er way through mud and slime.

Note that the public-morality nonsense applies only to politicians; captains of industry may swap wives without being obliged to leave office, and of actors it seems positively expected that they should. Of course, those who are ex officio charged with the care of souls, like bishops, or with literally laying down the law, like judges, must observe certain rules that do not apply to the rest of us, because something real and important would be damaged if too many of them fell too conspicuously from grace. But that is the price a man pays for wearing a full-bottomed wig or lawn sleeves; who started the rumour that politicians are in a similar position, and whoever he was, why didn't he notice that it isn't true?

It is surely ironic beyond the dreams of the *Daily Telegraph* leader-writers that Britain, the originator of representative parliamentary government, should be afflicted more than any other nation with the claim that public men are different from private ones. Democracy wouldn't even work if that were true, if we selected our political representatives from some pool of special beings resembling Miss Beale and Miss Buss ('...are different from us'), for we must be able to see ourselves mirrored in our politicians; as I have said more than once, in a democracy we are *all* politicians, and the day we forget it will be a black day for us all.

One day we shall all grow out of it; we shall be able to see a domestic tragedy for no more and no less than what it is, and to evince no pretended surprise that it should have taken place around a politician. I don't know what the mass-circulation papers will do for a living then, but that is not my problem. Let us resolve to remember that the world and its inhabitants are not perfect, and are most unlikely to become perfect by next Friday, and to remember also that 'in the course of justice none of us should see salvation'. Meanwhile, it must remain true, alas, that people who live in glass houses should undress in the dark.

- Bernard Levin, *The Times*, 17.10.83, after Cecil Parkinson's downfall over the Sarah Keays affair

★ ☆ ★

Where I agree with the historian, Eric Hobsbawn, is in his insistence on the need for idealism. Asked if he regretted having been a communist, he replies:

'No, I don't think so. I know very well that the cause that I embraced has proved not to work. Perhaps I shouldn't have chosen it. But, on the other hand, if people don't have any ideal of a better world, then they have lost something. If the only ideal for men and women is the pursuit of personal happiness through the attainment of material assets, then humanity is a diminished species.'

Very true, Professor. Though I am inclined to repeat the two words with which President Coolidge dismissed an agricultural delegation grumbling about the bad times: 'Get religion.'

• Paul Johnson, reviewing *The New Century* by Eric Hobsbawm with Antonio Polito, *Spectator*, 22.4.00

★ ☆ ★

I remember the first time John Kennedy met Nikita Khrushchev – and the last. It was in Vienna in June of 1961 and the Soviet Chairman came to the American Embassy in his ice-cream coloured suit and his broad smile. Kennedy had met him on the front stairs, in front of hundreds of photographers and reporters and the imp in him had not resisted a small joke at the Soviet leader's expense. Pointing to a medal affixed to Khrushchev's chest, the President asked him what it was. 'It is the Lenin Peace Prize,' Khrushchev responded. 'Well,' said Kennedy smilingly, 'don't do anything here so they'll take it away from you.' Two days after a tough exchange, there were no smiles when the two men parted. 'It's going to be a cold winter,' Kennedy told Khrushchev referring to their conversations over Berlin.

I remember too the days of the Cuban Missile Crisis. I remember the President's military aide coming around and handing me a sealed envelope. They were instructions for my wife should the American Government have to disappear to a secret location because of an imminent Soviet nuclear attack. For 10 days, I left my office barely three hours a day to sleep at a nearby hotel.

My assistant slept on the floor of my office, the secretaries in the White House bomb shelter. And I remember Robert Kennedy exploding at a meeting of the National Security Council when somebody suggested a sneak air attack on Cuba to take out the Soviet missile sites. 'I will not be a party to an American Pearl Harbor,' he shouted at the men around the table.

There is no purpose now in trying to imagine how much would be different if John Kennedy had lived. He did not. It is sufficient to understand that 10 years after his death, his spirit lives on, a spirit characterised by a quotation of George Bernard Shaw that was one of the President's favourites: 'Some people see things as they are and ask why? I dream dreams that never were and ask why not?'

• Pierre Salinger, Press Secretary to John F Kennedy, *Guardian*, 20.11.73

★ ☆ ★

When asked if he had any skeletons in his cupboard, English MP and diarist Alan Clark said: 'Dear boy, I can hardly close the door.'

• Steve Boggan, *Independent*, 8.9.99

★ ☆ ★

A device known as an induction loop set was issued to reporters at international conferences and meetings to enable the reporters to listen to the opening ceremonies. But it also plugged us into some of the informal chit-chat between political leaders not meant to be overheard by the Press. Before the opening of a Commonwealth Conference, the British Prime Minister James Callaghan was performing admirable feats of memory with President Kaunda of Zambia sitting next to him. He was recalling a meeting of the Fabian Society which they had both attended in 1957, along with Mr Harry Nkumbala, who used to be Mr Kaunda's rival Zambian leader.

It Takes All Sorts

'What happened to Harry Nkumbala?' wondered Mr Callaghan. 'Is he still alive?' Mr Kaunda, less audible, indicated that he was but was suffering from some nasty disability. 'That is a great pity,' said Mr Callaghan. 'He is not the first one.'

• Michael Leapman, *The Times*, 9.6.77

★ ☆ ★

It is the folly of too many to mistake the echo of a London coffee house for the voice of the Kingdom.

• Jonathan Swift in *The Conduct of Allies*

★ ☆ ★

Herbert Morrison, the British Cabinet Minister, asked Vicky, the cartoonist, why he made his legs so thin. 'To save ink,' replied Vicky.

★ ☆ ★

He always looked as if he were on the verge of being found out.

• Rebecca West about Harold Wilson, British Prime Minister

★ ☆ ★

He is an over-ripe banana, yellow outside, squishy within.'

• Reginald Paget about British Prime Minister, Anthony Eden.

★ ☆ ★

Politics is perhaps the only profession for which no preparation is thought necessary.

Robert Louis Stevenson, 1882

★ ☆ ★

Democracy means simply the bludgeoning of the people, by the people, for the people.

• Oscar Wilde

★ ☆ ★

Something unpleasant is coming when men are anxious to tell the truth.

• Benjamin Disraeli

★ ☆ ★

Every pressure group provokes resistance from another pressure group.

• Anon

★ ☆ ★

Lord Castlerose, gossip columnist of Lord Beaverbrook's *Sunday Express*, was known for his buffoonery and extravagant behaviour. Meeting him on a golf course, Nancy Cunard asked, 'What is your handicap?' 'Drink and debauchery' was his reply.

★ ☆ ★

Well done to the *Daily Sport* for its coverage on the death of Sir John Gielgud, one of England's greatest actors. The obituary in yesterday's paper was headlined: 'Butler in Dudley Moore film dies'.

• Peterborough, *Daily Telegraph*, 2.6.00

★ ☆ ★

Utopia is an island of complete equality. It's Communist. Everyone works nine hours a day – six in the morning to three in the afternoon – everyone has to have a trade. You're not allowed to travel without a licence – if you do you're made a slave. The slaves are criminals. Thomas More hears this from a traveller called Raphael Hythloday, who says he's been there. It's beyond the horizon of Europe, and the word 'Utopia' itself is a bit of a puzzle. More made it up, and it actually means 'no place'. But it's apparent that Hythloday, describing the island of Utopia, already thinks it's the best place, an ideal place. And that division has really tormented the history of Utopias right through: is it pure fantasy, impossible, or is it an ideal that we really could aim for? I don't know whether *Utopia* is a funny book. I find students laugh a lot at the idea in it that when you marry you should see your wife naked beforehand, in the presence of some grave matron. Well, it's not very different from trial marriages, from living together, which everyone accepts now.

• John Carey, *Independent on Sunday* Magazine, 26.12.99

26 Journalists Fill White Spaces

press and journalists

The *New Yorker* once tried to buy a chapter from my *Life of Jesus*. I was thrilled. A month before publication I received a call from someone who said he was the 'fact checker' who wanted to make sure the article had been thoroughly 'lawyered'. He spoke as if writs could easily arrive from Pontius Pilate or Judas Iscariot any minute.

I tried to explain that the New Testament, however venerable a collection of writings, does not contain any 'facts' in the modern sense of the word. It was a case, as in Stalin's show trials, of 'everything is true except the facts'. After more conversations like this, my extract never got published.

• A N Wilson, *Evening Standard* 10.7.98

★ ☆ ★

Hello and farewell. After nearly a year of this column I've run out of things to talk about. I do not own a charming pet, whose daily escapades can be chronicled astutely for the discerning reader. I am not beset by builders who fail to turn up and then pour concrete into my swimming-pool. And I have no child to exploit for columnic purposes. These benefits are denied to me, and I have had to make do with a sadly depleted litany of ever narrowing subjects. I found myself writing about Jeffrey Archer the other week and I knew it was time to stop.

The trouble is that I do not hold spectacularly strong opinions on almost any subject you care to mention. My view on most matters could be summarised as, 'Don't know really. It's all right, I suppose.' This attitude encompasses basketball, puff pastry and a lot of other stuff in between. And I think you need strong opinions at your disposal if you're writing an opinion piece. That's my opinion, anyway. And I hold it vehemently.

• Paul Merton, *Sunday Telegraph*, 26.12.99

★ ☆ ★

Newspapers have degenerated so far now that you can rely upon them absolutely.

• Oscar Wilde

★ ☆ ★

What exactly *was* Diana, the artist formerly known as Princess? During her anorexic period, she and Karen Carpenter were the only two famous people whose pictures could fit on to the spine of a CD cover...but St Squidgy, Our Lady of Versace, never sang.

She and Mother Teresa were the original ho-spice girls...but Diana never healed anyone. In truth, she was nothing more than a brood mare crossed with a clothes horse, picked to produce thoroughbred offspring and keep her gob shut in return for occasional 24-carat sugar lumps, and on her tombstone should be written this: Some are born great. Some achieve greatness. And some hire great PR companies.

I wrote the above lines a week after Diana died, intending to include them in a review of *that* funeral. But they never appeared in print, not because of censorship by the *Evening Standard* but because of a much more insidious form of suppression: self-censorship. Yes, I was one of the many cowardly journalists in desperate need of a spine-transplant during the first days of September; but at least I had enough sense of self-preservation to write nothing at all about her, thereby sparing me the ignominy of being quoted on last night's deliciously clinical autopsy of that shameful, frenzied, media-led period, 'Diana: the Mourning After' (Channel 4).

• Victor Lewis-Smith, *Evening Standard*, 28.8.98.

★ ☆ ★

Peregrine Worsthorne criticised Britain's newspapers for being too clever, not too dumb, in the new edition of the *Spectator*. To his credit, he offers an illustrative anecdote about his own earlier career on the *Daily Telegraph* when he was sent to cover an African coup d'état.

'Instead of keeping my eyes open in the bus on the way from the airport to the city centre, I had mine buried in some learned tome about the country's history. As a result, unlike the tabloid reporters on the bus – few if any of whom in those days had a degree – I failed to notice the decapitated corpses lying by the roadside.'

• Pandora, *Independent*, 20.11.98

★ ☆ ★

The Alonquin's Round Table was born by accident in June of 1919, when a group of journalists gathered to fête the return of the *New York Times* drama critic Alexander Woollcott from his service in World War I. The venue was such a success that the group decided to meet on a regular basis.

The quick-barbs-and-repartee lunches became so renowned that other writers, columnists and out-of-town curiosity seekers soon began dining at the hotel, hoping to overhear *bons mots* filtering over from the self-congratulatory supernumeraries.

By 1932, the Round Table had disbanded, the core group having moved on to writing for Hollywood or careers in radio. Years later, Dorothy Parker would describe the Round Table as 'that not particularly brave little band that hid its nakedness of heart and mind under the out-of-date garment of a sense of humour.'

• Joseph Olsham, *Daily Express* Colour Supplement, 31.1.99

★ ☆ ★

There was an editorial conference [at the *Spectator*] once a week; it was a small family affair, and more often than not attended by Peter Fleming, who was theatre critic and much else. He would drive up from Nettlebed to 99 Gower Street in a Rolls-Royce station-wagon, the coachwork designed by himself. 'What do you need all that space for?' I asked him. 'I must have something I can put a stag in.' Fair enough.

• Recalling his days on the editorial staff of the post-war *Spectator*, E C Hodgkin, *Spectator*, 6.1.96

★ ☆ ★

At yesterday's memorial service for the late Charles Wintour, Lord Jenkins recalled the story of Wintour – then editor of the *Evening Standard* – interviewing a bright young Cambridge graduate for a job.

'Are you interested in politics?' Wintour asked.

'Very,' answered the young man, now known to us as Sir Tom Stoppard.

'Then who,' asked Wintour, 'is Home Secretary?'

Long pause. Stoppard replied: 'I am interested, not obsessed.'

• Peterborough, *Daily Telegraph*, 14.12.99

★ ☆ ★

I use the internet every day and use e-mail voraciously, so I'm a techno fan. But I will never love a computer like I love a newspaper – and I don't believe the vast majority of my readers will either.

Let's flip the debate on its head. Imagine an entirely computerised world where paper has not been invented. One day a bright lad stumbles on a stunning new invention, creating, from a piece of wood, something he calls paper. It is soft but very durable, and can be recycled easily and used to print cheaply in unlimited quantity. He tells a few mates, who initially laugh at him. Then he offers them a copy of the *Mirror* in paper form. 'Hey, this is good,' they cry. No phones, no wires, no batteries, no dodgy screens, no slow systems. You don't need a £1,000 machine to access it, and it only costs 32p. You can tear bits out, screw it into a ball, pass sections to others, even have your fish and chips out of it. 'I tell you what,' one says, 'this will really catch on. Computers will be dead in five years.'

• Piers Morgan, *Guardian*, 6.12.99

★ ☆ ★

A letter in which George Bernard Shaw said he valued sex 'as highly as a piece of plum cake' was purchased yesterday for £18,000 as a gift for a woman who bakes an excellent plum cake.

The buyer, who wished to remain anonymous, saw the sale advertised on the Internet and decided that the letter would make the perfect gift for his girlfriend's cake-baking mother.

The letter was discovered recently in a cupboard 104 years after Shaw wrote to Laura Ormiston Chant, a social reformer and campaigner against prostitution.

The two struck up a correspondence after he criticised her revelation that prostitutes were soliciting at a theatre in Leicester Square, London, which had prompted its closure.

In his letter of 17 November 1894 Shaw expressed sympathy for prostitutes, saying that he respected their trade 'as I am bound to respect that lower depth of prostitution by which I have for so many years earned my own living: to wit, journalism.'

• Louise Jury, *Independent*, 3.12.98

★ ☆ ★

'It's very difficult to make a film that can portray the fashion industry properly, because it is so bizarre,' says Alexandra Shulman, the editor of British *Vogue*. 'The extraordinary mix of characters, the massive egos at play, the huge amounts of money at stake and the beauty of the women involved make it unlike any other industry on earth.'

Only this month, Shulman was having a meeting to arrange the magazine's next cover. A big-name photographer was to fly to somewhere exotic, at great expense, and shoot a hot new model in return for a preposterously large fee. Shulman decided that, just for a change, she'd like a smiling cover girl this time. Suddenly, the team turned ashen and the project seemed to fall apart like a delicately balanced house of cards. Why? The model in question, Shulman was curtly informed, doesn't do smiles. 'She doesn't smile!' exclaims Shulman, still incredulous a few weeks after the event. 'I mean, that's pretty mad, isn't it?'

• Simon Mills, *Sunday Times*, 14.5.00

★ ☆ ★

Although Bob Kane, creator of Batman, had always wanted to be a purely funny cartoonist, there were pre-echoes of the sinister shadows of the batman that was to come. When Peter and his little buddy Tinymite (Batman and Robin?) landed on the Moon they came face to horrid face with Zula, supreme ruler of the lunar men: 'a monstrosity because of his one eye and devil horns, a madman with a burning desire to become ruler of the entire world.' Speaking in irregular lettering as befitted an alien Zula the Great hypnotises Peter and ropes him beneath a steel roller studded with sharp spikes. 'Heh! Heh!' he hehs. Suddenly a cuckoo-clock chirps the hour of four: 'So sorry,' says Zula, 'Tea-time! Won't you join me in a cup of tea?' *To be continued...*

Kane was one of the few cartoonists to retain rights in his characters. 'Not complete rights, just a part, but enough to ensure my name was always on the strip whether I drew it or not, and to be certain I was given reasonable credits on spin-offs.' This meant the two Columbia film serials, the ABC Television series, and the more recent cinema features.

I asked Kane how he felt when young academics wrote deep books analysing the psychology of his Batman hero. 'I smile,' he said. 'I can't even spell psychology.'

• Denis Gifford, *Independent*, 9.11.98

★ ☆ ★

Evelyn Irons, who died in May, 2000, was the first woman war correspondent to be awarded the Croix de Guerre, and the first woman since Grace Darling to receive the Stanhope Gold Medal of the Royal Humane Society. A journalist of outstanding courage and resourcefulness, she drank Hitler's wine, attended Marilyn Monroe's marriage to Arthur Miller and beat 40 male correspondents to the story of the 1954 Guatemalan revolution by hiring a mule on which to make the risky border crossing (an act that caused a rival correspondent's disconsolate editor to cable his man, 'Offget arse, onget donkey soonest').

• *The Times*, 11.5.00

★ ☆ ★

When Randolph Churchill sued the newspaper, *The People*, who had called him a 'paid hack', he was asked by the newspaper's defence barrister if he had not referred to the paper as 'The lowest mongrel cur in Fleet Street'? Churchill replied: 'That remark arose out of the saying "dog doesn't eat dog". If you use metaphors from the canine world you naturally use the metaphor drawn from the same world, otherwise you complicate the issue and don't carry your audience with you.'

• Court report of trial

★ ☆ ★

A writer sent an unsolicited short story to the *New Yorker* magazine and received back a rejection slip which read: 'Sorry. Too much like us.'

★ ☆ ★

'When you finish a story,' wrote Abe Rosenthal, editor of the *New York Times* in his last column, 'I would say (to a reporter), read it, substitute your name for the subject's. If you say, well, it would make me miserable, make my wife cry, but has no innuendo, no unattributed pejorative remarks, no slap in the face for the joy of slapping, it's news, not gutter gossip, and as a reporter I know the writer was fair, then give it to the copy desk. But if not, try again – we don't want to be your cop.'

• *New York Times*, November, 1999

★ ☆ ★

Life, real honest-to-goodness life, with murders and catastrophes and fabulous inheritances, happens almost exclusively in newspapers.

• Anon

27 The Wonder Of It All

profundities and religion

A neurosis is a secret you don't know you're keeping.

• Kenneth Tynan, Theatre Critic

★ ☆ ★

Everyone fears they are a joke which other people will one day get.

• Martin Amis, quoted in the *Guardian*

★ ☆ ★

A pal of mine claims to have done very well in first-year philosophy on the basis of an exam in which, in response to the question, 'Why is there something rather than nothing?' he replied: 'Because nothing is something.'

• Arthur O'Neill, *Philosophers Magazine*, Autumn 1998, quoted in the *Guardian* Editor magazine, 28.11.98

★ ☆ ★

It's amazing how complete is the delusion that beauty is goodness.

• Tolstoy

★ ☆ ★

Lucy, Lucy, my dear child, don't tear your frock: tearing frocks is not of itself a proof of genius, but write as your mother writes, act as your mother acts; be frank, loyal, affectionate, simple, honest, and then integrity or laceration of frock is of little import.

And Lucy, dear child, mind your arithmetic. You know, in the first sum of yours I ever saw, there was a mistake. You had carried two (as a cab is licensed to do) and you ought, dear Lucy, to have carried but one. Is this a trifle? What would life be without arithmetic, but a scene of horrors?

You are going to Boulogne, the city of debts, peopled by men who never understood arithmetic; by the time you return, I shall probably have received my first paralytic stroke, and shall have lost all recollection of you; therefore I now give you my parting advice. Don't marry anybody who has not a tolerable understanding of arithmetic and a thousand a year, and God bless you, dear child.

- Sydney Smith, writing on 22 July 1835 to fourteen-year-old Miss Lucy Austin (1821–69). He was a local curate. From Oxford Book of Letters (p.233) ed. Frank and Anita Kermode

★ ☆ ★

In matters of grave importance, style, not sincerity, is the vital thing.

- Oscar Wilde, quoted in the *Independent*

★ ☆ ★

Puritanism is the haunting fear that someone somewhere might be happy.

- Mark Twain

★ ☆ ★

If you haven't got talent or genius, money is the next best thing.

- Milton Shulman

★ ☆ ★

Does one want to be appreciated as an amusing, charming, modest nonentity or a hard-working, insensitive success?

• Anon

★ ☆ ★

What people say behind your back is your standing in the community in which you live.

• Anon

★ ☆ ★

What fools call loneliness, wise men know as solitude.

• Chinese proverb

★ ☆ ★

Where is the man who has uncontrovertible evidence of the truth of all that he holds or the falsehood of all that he condemns?

• John Locke, 1687

★ ☆ ★

It is hard to believe that a man is telling the truth when you know you would lie if you were in his place.

• H L Mencken

★ ☆ ★

It is a terrible thing for a man to find out suddenly that all his life he has been speaking nothing but the truth.

• Oscar Wilde

★ ☆ ★

It Takes All Sorts

An intellectual is someone whose mind watches itself.
• Albert Camus

★ ☆ ★

To a toad what is beauty? A female with two pop eyes, a wide mouth, yellow belly and spotted back.
• Voltaire

★ ☆ ★

You can quite easily propose a logical solution to something and at the same time hope in your heart of hearts that it won't work out.
• Luigi Pirandello

★ ☆ ★

The optimist proclaims we live in the best of all possible worlds and the pessimist fears this is true.
• Anon

★ ☆ ★

Whenever a friend succeeds, a little something in me dies.
• Gore Vidal

★ ☆ ★

There's something wrong, if you're always right.
• Anon

★ ☆ ★

Any philosophy that can be put in a nutshell, belongs there.
• Anon

★ ☆ ★

There may be said to be two classes of people in the world: those who constantly divide the people of the world into two classes and those who don't.

• Robert Benchley

★ ☆ ★

Most general statements are false, including this one.

• Anon

★ ☆ ★

People talk because it is more manageable than silence.

• Anon

★ ☆ ★

Talk to a man about himself and he will listen for hours.

• Benjamin Disraeli

★ ☆ ★

Of all the lovely sounds on earth
The song of birds, rain's anodyne
The sweetest is the human voice:
Bewitching, undulating – mine!

• Leslie Millichamp

★ ☆ ★

Paul Merton says he began to reject the tenets of Catholicism well before his teens. 'All those extremes,' he says. 'To be told that there is either eternal bliss, walking around the clouds playing table tennis with Mozart and Cary Grant, or eternal damnation where you have to light Hitler's cigars – it does give you something to kick against.'

• Simon Garfield, *Guardian*, 29.8.98

★ ☆ ★

All proofs or disproofs that we tender
Of His existence are returned
Unopened to the sender.

• From *Friday's Child* by W H Auden

★ ☆ ★

The Vatican, which ten days ago decreed that God was not to be imagined as 'an old man with a white beard', will this week seek to recast the image of Satan, arguing that the Church needs a 'more subtle and sophisticated' definition of evil for the Millennium.

Definitions of 'demonic possession' and the rituals for dealing with it have largely remained unaltered since Pope Paul V (1605–21) issued the *Rituale Romanum* in 1614. It was revised under Leo XIII (1878–1903) but not substantially changed.

According to Vatican officials, under the new rituals priests will be encouraged not to refer any longer to the Prince of Darkness, the Accursed Dragon, the Foul Spirit, the Satanic Power or the Master of Deceit. Instead the formulas refer more vaguely to 'the cause of evil'.

Both Old and New Testaments refer to Beelzebub, the Evil One, or Satan, with the Devil often depicted as Lucifer, a rebel angel expelled from Heaven, a theme taken up in Milton's epic poem *Paradise Lost*. The Revelation of St John (xii.7) describes 'war in Heaven between the angels' (led by Michael) and 'the Dragon, that ancient serpent who led the whole world astray whose name is the Devil, or Satan'.

Jesus cast out demons in several famous New Testament passages, and St Mark (i.13) and St Matthew (iv.1-11) both record that Jesus was 'tempted by Satan' during his 40 days and 40 nights in the wilderness.

But some modern theologians regard the depiction of Satan as a reptilian beast with cloven hooves, wings and a tail, as a medieval invention, and prefer St Augustine's definition of evil as 'the absence of good'.

• Richard Owen, *The Times*, 25.1.99

★ ☆ ★

Sir Ian McKellen, the actor and defender of homosexual rights, has caused a stir by tearing a page from a Bible in his one-man show at the Royal Lyceum Theatre in Edinburgh. It came from the book of Leviticus, and includes the sentence: 'Thou shalt not lie with mankind as with womankind: it is an abomination' (18:22). This has often been cited by conservative Christians to justify their condemnation of homosexual relationships, especially those within the Church of England. Sir Ian revealed that he removes the same page from hotel Bibles on his travels, conjuring up an image of the great actor, no sooner unpacked than setting to work with a razor. He urged his audience to do the same.

Homosexuals are not alone in being outlawed by Leviticus: so are sexual relations with both a woman and her daughter, with a wife's sister, a neighbour's wife and just about any form of relative. Death is recommended for all transgressors. The same intolerance is on view a chapter later, in which among those listed as unsuited to the priesthood are anyone blind, lame, disfigured or deformed, hunchbacked or dwarfed, or anyone with festering and running sores or damaged testicles.

In short, if all those insulted by the Old Testament were to follow Sir Ian's example, hotel Bibles would look as if they had been through a shredder. Homosexuals are not alone in bearing Leviticus a legitimate grudge. Silence is probably the best policy, but argument is preferable to vandalism, however selective it may be.

• Leader, *Independent*, 30.11.94

★ ☆ ★

Crime has become so pervasive in America that even churches are now producing pistol-packing preachers to protect their collection plates and religious icons. The bulge on the hip of Rev. O D Dempsey of the Upper Park Avenue Baptist church in Harlem conceals nothing more nor less than a very formidable pistol.

'Why am I packing a pistol?' says the Rev. Dempsey, after the Sunday morning service. 'Because it's like Dodge City out there on the streets. We've had people come right into the church and steal anything they can find that's not nailed down. They even took the organ once,' he said mournfully. 'I mean – OK, typewriters, TV sets – but the organ! No, No.'

Rev. Dempsey is no exception in the United States. A number of clerics have been murdered, and now a lot of clergymen have given up depending on the Lord alone. In Pittsburg recently a Catholic priest shot and killed a 19-year-old thief. 'Turn the other cheek is fine,' says Rev. Charles Angel, a minister from Manhattan's Upper Westside. 'But that means getting ripped off, beaten up and mugged. If you've got a decent-sized church, you've got yourself two or three grand in unmarked bills. So what are you gonna do? Hand over the collection to them?'

• Roderich Gilchrist, *Daily Mail*, June 1977

★ ☆ ★

People can say what they like about Christianity; but the religious system that produced green Chartreuse can never really die.

★ ☆ ★

God is very economical. He wastes nothing.

• Sir Ralph Richardson

★ ☆ ★

Father Agnelius Andrew was the BBC's adviser on Roman Catholic religious affairs. Planning a programme on the after-life a producer wrote to him asking how he could find out what was the official Roman Catholic view of heaven and hell. Father Andrew replied with a letter containing just one word: 'Die.'

★ ☆ ★

Matthew Arnold, the British writer and critic, who died in 1888, was a severe moralist with severe standards of morality and intellectual prowess. Hearing of his death, the American writer Robert Louis Stevenson said; 'Poor Matthew – he's gone to Heaven, no doubt, but he won't like God.'

28 What's So Funny About Sex?

sex

During a lecture, Alfred Kinsey asked a female student to name the body part that can enlarge a hundred times. She replied: 'You have no right to ask me such a question in a mixed class.' Kinsey coldly riposted: 'I was referring to the pupil of the eye; and you, young lady, are in for a terrible disappointment.'

• Jonathan Gathorne-Hardy, quoted by Val Hennessy, *Daily Mail*, 15.8.98

★ ☆ ★

A celibates' club set up by 214 women in Dortmund, Germany, six years ago has been forced to close. There is only one member left who is not pregnant or married.

• *Sunday Times*, 25.10.98

★ ☆ ★

In the *New York Times*, Maureen Dowd drew a comparison between Monica Lewinsky and the late Pamela Harriman. 'With their porcelain complexions and pillowy figures, both Pamela and Monica zeroed in on powerful men, unfettered by any twinges of conscience about wives, enveloping their quarry with rapt gazes, flattery and sex that catered to male wishes and fantasies,' she wrote.

What shocking things to say about an English aristocrat and daughter-in-law of Winston Churchill who ended her career as

American ambassador in Paris! But Ms Dowd at least recognises a substantial class difference between the woman who helped Bill Clinton to the White House with her fund-raising and the one who brought him low. 'The problem with this scandal is not illicit sex,' she wrote. 'The problem is that we need a better class of illicit sex.'

But what both the above examples seem to show is how little there is left to say.

• Alexander Chancellor, *The Times*, 13.10.98

★ ☆ ★

'Of course, this isn't the first case I've come across of a man seeking sexual gratification from his vacuum cleaner,' Public Safety Director Louis Napoletano told reporters in Long Branch, New Jersey, 'but this guy obviously didn't know his model very well. If he had, he'd have known that right under where the hose attaches, there's a revolving blade for pushing the dust into the collection bag.'

Napoletano was speaking the day after a fifty-one-year-old man had been rushed to the Monmouth Medical Center with a severed penis and severe blood loss. When police officers responded to his 911 call, they burst into his house and found him lying in a pool of blood. At first, he told them that he had cut himself shaving. Then he said someone had broken in and stabbed him in the crotch, but the vacuum cleaner was covered in blood and one of the officers found the amputated tip of his penis in the dust bag, so it was pretty obvious what had happened.

'We got him to the medical center as soon as possible, and doctors tried to reattach the severed part, but without success. This morning, the man admitted to us that he'd got drunk while his wife was away, and had decided to seek sexual pleasure from the vacuum suction. It just goes to show, you should do what the manufacturers say: always read your appliance handbook before switching it on.'

• *Associated Press*, 13.5.98. Quoted by Victor Lewis-Smith in *Private Eye*

★ ☆ ★

One summer day in 1772, the Marquis de Sade, sporting a plumed hat, a vest of marigold-yellow satin with matching breeches and a gold-knobbed cane, organised a party in the room of a prostitute in Marseilles, where his valet had assembled four girls for his pleasure. In the frantic hours that followed, he indulged in sodomy with his servant while successively copulating with, whipping and being whipped by the prostitutes, to whom he had fed aphrodisiac sweets that later made them quite sick.

This exploit led to his conviction by a Marseilles court for sodomy and attempt to poison. With his wife, Pélagie's connivance, he eluded the authorities by fleeing to Italy in the company of his sister-in-law.

Sade's once adoring mother-in-law, upon learning that he had deflowered her favourite daughter, became his fiercest enemy. He was incarcerated, at her instigation, in the fortress of Miolans, in Savoy. Yet once again Pélagie rushed to his rescue. She spent weeks in a neighbouring village, dressed as a man, trying to arrange her husband's getaway.

After his successful escape – through the only unbarred window in the prison – Sade fled to Italy for the winter. By this time, Pélagie had sent the children – all of them still under six years of age – back to Paris to be brought up by Madame de Montreuil.

• Francine de Plessix Gray, reviewing her own book *At Home with the Marquis de Sade*, *Sunday Telegraph*, 3.1.99

* * *

I have good 'scientific' reasons for thinking that H J Eysenck may be more worried now than formerly about the acceptability of his brand of behaviourism. I have compared the number of 'defensive' statements in his new book, *Psychology is about People* (I define as 'defensive' any statement in which an anxious general reference to critics of behaviourism is made), with the number appearing in *Fact and Fiction in Psychology* and *Sense and Nonsense in Psychology*, two of Eysenck's other 'popular' early books. There is an increase of nearly 40 per cent. There is even a chapter with the title, 'Don't shoot the behaviourist; he is doing his best.' (I scored ten for this.)

In case all this seems more like heavy-handed humour than science, then I can recommend for those who welcome a lighter touch, the chapter in his book on 'The uses and abuses of pornography', in which Eysenck clears away all that evaluative clutter which has collected around the concept of pornography by the simple device of creating a pornography index (P). When assessing a passage you score one point for a reference to 'lips or shoulders', one for 'breast', and eight for 'sexual parts proper'. When actions are being assessed one simply multiplies the noun score by two if the action is manual, or by four if the action is oral. So 'kissing the nipples' is five points for nipples, multiplied by four for kissing, to make a score of 20 quite high really; I'm sorry if my example excited you. The elaboration of this method eventually allows one to compare Henry Miller, the *Kama Sutra* and D H Lawrence.

• Laurie Taylor, reviewing *Psychology is about People* by H J Eysenck, *New Society*, 22.6.72

★ ☆ ★

Chastity is the most unnatural of the sexual perversions.

• Anon

★ ☆ ★

A musical condom which plays a stirring tune while couples make love has been invented in Germany. A tiny microchip implanted in the tip of the condom offers a selection of three tunes. They are Love Me Tender, the Wedding March and the German equivalent of For He's A Jolly Good Fellow. The inventor, Karl Wiegand from Dortmund, has been granted a patent for the invention.

• *Evening Standard*, 8.4.99

★ ☆ ★

Having sex is one of the reasons for reincarnation – the other eight reasons are unimportant.

• Henry Miller, quoted in *OK!* magazine, 27.8.99

★ ☆ ★

To be a gigolo – a dancing partner or escort of an older woman – is a hell of an honourable profession. Or used to be. In fact, some of my best friends were gigolos. Starting with Porfirio Rubirosa, the legendary playboy, pistolero, polo player, diplomat and lover of beautiful women. He was my mentor and best man when I married my first wife. Rubi was a modern Robin Hood. He took from rich women and spent it on younger poor ones. Now what could be fairer than that? Even those envious types of the scummy *Guardian* would have to agree. Rubi practised socialism in countries where it was a very dirty word. Like the Dominican Republic, or Ciudad Trujillo, as it was back when he ran off with Flor de Oro Trujillo, daughter of strongman Raphael Leonidas Trujillo.

After Flor, and a permanent diplomatic post to Paris, Rubi married Doris Duke. He got Paris as a goodbye gift from Flor's father, but no cash. La Duke provided walking around moolah, plus a string of polo ponies. Soon after he married Danielle Darieux, France's most beautiful film star. It was true love, and it lasted throughout the war. When the cash ran out, Rubi married Barbara Hutton, and in 73 days got an aeroplane, 55 suits, £3 million – this was 1953 – and more polo ponies. His last wife, Odile, had not a penny but was among the sexiest and most beautiful girls in Paris. She was to become his widow. He died on the morning of 6 July 1965, having won the polo French Open and having spent the night celebrating with a member of the losing team, yours truly. He hit a tree while driving home in his Ferrari. A perfect death for a gigolo-cum-sportsman-cum-playboy.

• Taki, *Spectator*, 1.4.00

★ ☆ ★

Thomas Allen, the great British baritone, and I agreed that the original Don Giovanni must have been very selfish and probably not all that interesting. Oscar Wilde once said that the man who goes about trying to seduce every woman he meets is boring and vulgar. The really romantic lady-killer is the man, like Byron, who says to women, go away, I don't need you, my life is complete without you.

• Petronella Wyatt, *Spectator*, 1.4.00

★ ☆ ★

Adrian Daintrey, the painter who died in 1988, shared Augustus John's whole admiration for the opposite sex, many of whom showed their appreciation in the most practical manner. Daintrey ended his days in the Charterhouse, where to the end he was visited by many charming young women. I have lost an old friend, and I do not doubt that Daintrey's passing will bring a tear to the eye of more than one lady of quality and black bus conductress.

• Anthony Powell, *Daily Telegraph Book of Obituaries*, edited by Hugh Massingberd

★ ☆ ★

Jokes are an important factor in sex appeal. Men have absolutely no idea what makes other men attractive to women – but it's clear laughter is the weapon of the male whose sex appeal may not be immediately obvious. My friend George Melly, no longer young and dressed in what appears to be the wardrobe of a touring production of *Guys and Dolls*, can attract any woman by making her laugh.

Laughter is essential to a woman's appeal also, which rules out many models who suck in their cheeks, don't make jokes and take their beauty seriously.

Time has passed and many whom I knew as waifs have become extraordinarily attractive women in their 50s, wonderfully free of another great anti-aphrodisiac – political correctness.

They don't cover their glasses with their hands when you offer them a drink. They don't flap their hands in the air if anyone lights a cigarette within 50 yards of them. They don't regard animals as in every way morally and spiritually superior to human beings or foxes as strict upholders of animal rights.

Tired of endless stories about middle-aged men who leave their equally middle-aged wives for beautiful young girls, I wrote a tale about a man who leaves his stunning young wife for a drinking, smoking politically incorrect Old Labour beauty of half a century. I hope this will be an encouragement to all such women, of all political persuasions.

There is a great deal of sex appeal in lines of laughter at the corners of the eyes, put there by years of living life to the full and enjoying it.

• John Mortimer, *Daily Mail*, 16.3.99

★ ☆ ★

Masochism entered the vocabulary a hundred years ago. The early Austrian sexologist Richard von Krafft-Ebing was responsible for giving us masochism, alongside a wide collection of other secular sins, including beast-defilement, necrophilia, and the other lurid, often ludicrous categories that fill out his extensive encyclopedia of the perversions, *Psychopathia Sexualis*.

He named the new discovery after a well known contemporary of his, who lived in the same town, Graz, and had taught in the same university. Leopold von Sacher-Masoch was the author of novels involving powerful, temperamental women and sensitive, strategic men. For Krafft-Ebing, masochism was a masculine perversion that involved the enjoyment of being dominated by a woman.

In other words, even temporary gender-role reversals were to be ruled out of court, exiled to the twilight world of the perversions. It would have made absolutely no sense to this psychiatrist to suggest that masochism was applicable to women. For him, feminine submission to the male was normal behaviour. (The same view, elaborated and sophisticated, appeared later on in Freud, the founder of psychoanalysis: masochism was a perversion that only applied to the male.) Feminism, of course, changed all that, giving women equality in an unexpected area and yet another thing to worry about.

• Anita Phillips, *Independent*, 20.3.99

★ ☆ ★

In his diary dated April 10, 1973, Kenneth Tynan, the brilliant British theatre critic, recounts a weekend he and his wife, Elaine Dundy, spent at Notley, the home of Lord Olivier and Vivien Leigh in 1955. 'I had written pretty devastating things about Vivien, which Larry had deeply resented... Vivien herself seemed almost excited by them, and it was always she who took the initiative when we met. We arrived at Notley before lunch on Saturday. Larry was away in Spain where his brother had just died and would not be back until dinner. Vivien was vivacious, metallic and in a high manic state, talking endlessly with eyes unnaturally bright. There was a lot to drink at lunch after which Elaine and I retired for a siesta. Our room had separate beds.

'No sooner had I stripped to my Y-fronts and fallen asleep than I felt the sheet slowly turned back and a hand placed on my genitals. It was Vivien, naked under a peignoir. I began to respond and then suddenly thought how impossible it would be to cuckold a man I venerated under his own roof – a really cock-crinkling thought. I muttered it to Vivien, who pouted a bit, but eventually rose to her feet – and tip-toed across to Elaine's bed. I hastily dressed; as I left the room, Vivien and Elaine were sleepily embracing.'

• The Journals of Kenneth Tynan.

Vivien Leigh

29 Fast Food For The Eyes

television

TV encourages people to buy luxuries who can't afford necessities.

• TV Critic

★ ☆ ★

Dimwit Yanks are making a mockery of the American version of top telly quiz *Who Wants To Be A Millionaire?* The supposedly dumbed-down dollars dash is turning into a debacle – with contestants taking up to 20 minutes to answer the simplest of questions. One hopeless Homer left with NOTHING after being stumped by the $500 poser: 'Where is the Leaning Tower of Pisa?' He took ten minutes – from a choice of Italy, Spain, Germany or Japan – to transplant the famous Italian landmark to SPAIN! Another one took 16 minutes, using all his three lives by asking the audience, going 50-50 and phoning a friend, before winning $1,000 by picking John Prescott as Britain's Deputy Prime Minister. Yet his other options were Michael Caine, Richard Branson and Noel Gallagher!

• Nigel Pauley, *Daily Star*, 18.11.99

★ ☆ ★

Channel 4 has a peculiar way of sensing whether its programmes are in danger of offending taste and decency guidelines. Erect penises are a complete no-no in television land but of course during particularly saucy scenes a degree of tumescence is inevitable. How far can they go? Enter the 'angle of dangle' device.

Producers refer to a map of Scotland and in particular to the Mull of Kintyre. If the offending implement raises its head above the angle of the peninsula then it's out. If it doesn't, it's in. And with Nick Broomfield's film on fetishism on its way, such distinctions are going to be important.

• Diary, *Guardian*, 7.9.98

★ ☆ ★

A couple of years back, I tested the water of daytime TV by writing to the *Vanessa* show, then on ITV. 'Dear Vanessa team, I am a keen amateur inventor, who always tries to look on the positive side of life. I recently invented an illuminated condom that glows in the dark, but during use it began strobing so much that I could feel an epileptic fit coming on.

So, quick as a flash, I ran a bathful of water, chucked in my dirty washing and some Daz, then got in and had my *grand mal* in the tub, thus saving pounds on laundry bills! Invite me onto your show, and I'll show your viewers how to save money, too. Yours, Clarence Z Merkin.'

• Victor Lewis-Smith, *Evening Standard*, 19.1.99. (A merkin is a pubic wig.)

★ ☆ ★

Once in a while the question arises of why this column rarely concerns itself with television's most popular programmes – *Coronation Street*, *Heartbeat*, the National Lottery draw and so on. The answer is that the television column follows normal FT practice. The FT art critic does not concern himself with the Athena posters and elephant prints which are popular in so many homes, he deals with the better stuff. The books pages do not concentrate on airport paperbacks, sword and sorcery stories or detective novels, however popular they may be, but on serious biography, history and so on. There seems to be no curiosity about why FT coverage of those subjects depends upon quality rather than popularity, yet the question continues to arise with regard to television.

The fact is that a great deal of popular television is just as tedious, limited and demoralising as a great deal of popular art and literature. A week spent watching the popular programmes makes you wonder how dreadful most people's lives must be if such time-filling, uninspiring material is really what is wanted. Much of it continues year after year, decade after decade, virtually unchanged. Where popularity is concerned, familiarity is clearly priceless.

The demand that game shows and lifestyle series be treated with the same seriousness as *Cold War* or *Horizon* is part and parcel of that relativist craze which would have us believe that there is nothing to choose between rap music and Bach, and that it makes good sense for Britain to be turning out thousands of media studies graduates every year who can short-list Star Trek from memory but don't know the difference between a verb and a noun. It should surely be resisted.

• Christopher Dunkley, *Financial Times*, 11.11.98

★ ☆ ★

A television, intended to provide help for an orang-utan couple in St Petersburg Zoo, has turned them into telly addicts, the *Moscow Times* reported yesterday.

Monika and Rabu had failed to be model parents to their male baby, Ramon, so a Samsung executive, himself a new father, gave the set in the hope that educational videos might teach the orang-utans how to care for their offspring.

Rabu, the family's patriarch, has become so obsessed with the television which hangs outside his cage that he has started to ignore his mate who in turn is feeling rejected and miserable. Zoo officials have now curtailed viewing hours, in the hope that Rabu will regain his attentive nature and that Monika will resume her painting career, cast aside in favour of the box.

Rabu arrived in St Petersburg from Antwerp Zoo in 1997 and he and Monika had their offspring on November 20. However, being reared in captivity both parents had lost the nurturing instincts necessary to raise their baby, so he was removed to an incubator where he was fed and looked after by zoo staff.

The zoo plans to appeal to American primate centres for help. It also hopes to bring in human mothers to demonstrate their skills to the hapless orang-utan.

• Anna Blundy, *The Times*, 6.1.99

★ ☆ ★

As for the general loss of our minds, and even our hearts and souls, the biggest influence of the last century has been the growth of television.

Since the Fifties, when it was no more than an interesting novelty, this most evil and unnecessary of all the evil and unnecessary inventions of the 20th century has swollen into a blood-chilling monster, employing hundreds of thousands of people, some of them quite capable of useful work, in devising and broadcasting an unstoppable deluge of what is at best trivial, and at worst degenerate and wicked.

This power has corrupted the rest of the 'media', so that even once 'serious' newspapers are full of odious and degrading drivel, much of it concerned with the puffed-up, vainglorious television personalities themselves.

It has fostered criminality, brutality and cruelty, and pervaded the minds of the suggestible with images of polymorphous sexual hedonism.

It has softened the brains of supposedly great big grown-up politicians, public men and bishops, so that they will still be found arguing about sex education in schools when war, plague and famine rage all about them.

• Michael Wharton, *Daily Mail*, 29.4.00

★ ☆ ★

Tick where applicable. You are either: an addict, an insomniac, a couch potato, a cynic, an ambivalent [what's that?], a populist or a soap-a-holic. The BBC, the CIA Media Lab and the WGBH Viewing Lab have come up with new classifications for the television audience. Now, two things strike me about this – no, two and a half things. The half is a continued amazement at the job-creation possibilities in the new information stews. What on earth is a WGBH Viewing Lab operative, and did CIA Media Lab choose their name so that it would be easier to pick up sad gullible women in wine bars?

The first thing we can see from this list is how fantastically, gaspingly, dismissively patronising every single category is – an eye-rolling, nose-pinching sneer. With the exception of prison warders, I can't think of any profession that would publicly refer to its customers in such underclass terms. It's an endemic truth about television that it hates its audience; the ultimate horror for a Tristram is to be mistaken for the sort of person who might watch his programmes. Imagine a novelist who boasted he never read a book, or a theatre director who never saw a play. But in television there is a canteen culture of Us and Them: media patricians serving slack-jawed *Untermensch* plebs. Those insulting labels are as much about confirming the Tristrams' shaky self-belief as actually targeting programmes.

The second thing these categories tell us is that television, as it's conceived and made, is essentially in the business of repetition rather than innovation. Most new and original programmes happen by accident, or so late at night nobody's concentrating. By identifying the audience by what they already watch, the BBC implicitly admits that it plans to produce more of the same.

What Greg Dyke – the Director General of the BBC – needs to change more than anything at the BBC is the hothouse conceit that came up with these labels. He needs to employ programme-makers who make programmes for themselves. He needs to create a company that is proud not just of its global vastness and clout, but of its individual product. And I've a new set of audience labels the Tristrams might find useful. How about: the people who pay your mortgage, those who keep you off the dole queue, folk who make it possible for you to be sarkily superior in the Groucho, or how about simply 'sir' and 'madam?'

• A A Gill, *The Sunday Times*, 30.4.00

30 Fuck The Audience

theatre and playwrights

A woman once wrote to Harold Pinter to ask him to explain *The Birthday Party*. 'These are the points I do not understand: 1. Who are the two men? 2. Where did Stanley come from? 3. Were they all supposed to be normal? You will appreciate that without the answers to these questions I cannot fully understand your play.'

Pinter replied: 'These are the points I do not understand: 1. Who are you? 2. Where do you come from? 3. Are you supposed to be normal? You will appreciate that without the answers to these questions, I cannot fully understand your letter.'

Alan Ayckbourn, then a callow twenty-year-old playing Stanley in an early production of the play in Scarborough, also had the temerity to ask Pinter for some biographical details of the mysterious concert pianist. 'Mind your own fucking business,' he was told. 'Just say the lines.'

His refusal to explain, to seek the roots of his inspiration, can be frustrating for audiences. He doesn't care. 'Will the audience absorb the implications or not?' he once wrote to a bemused director. 'Ask the barber.' He was even more explicit in an interview in 1993. 'As a director I give the actors one note at the very end of the other notes, one note: fuck the audience. And every actor knows what I'm talking about. If you want the audience to love you, you're finished. When an audience is a good and intelligent audience, I like them as much as anybody does. But you've got to take a strong view, saying you're going to get what we're giving you, you're not going to get what you want. There has to be someone in charge of a theatrical enterprise, and it has to be the work itself.'

• Stephen Moss, *Guardian*, 4.9.99

★ ☆ ★

Half a century of reading plays suggests that I don't 'visualise' at all well. I *hear*, but I don't always see what is happening. 'Hello,' says the text, 'what have we here?' If one is a good play-reader one ought to know what the detective has spotted on the rug. I think *hearing* plays started with reading Shakes to myself at a tender age. In my family, next to the Bible, Shakespeare was the o'er-licensed reading fodder. My parents were Shakespeareans to the point of forming a Reading Society in which they hogged the best parts (i.e. when it was Antony and C, mother read C of course, but father read both A and Enobarbus. Others got lesser roles with one big line, 'What-ho, without!' If Bible reading led to troublesome questions about Jezebel, more redoubtable were the piping treble inquiries after a morning with *Measure for Measure*. What does 'unnatural whoreson' mean? Pause – but a child must be told truth of a kind. Grasping the nettle, a stern parent replies, 'Like Oscar Wilde, dear, *only worse!*'

• Philip Hope-Wallace, *Guardian*, 6.3.69

★ ☆ ★

Back in 1787 an actor called Cubitt undertook the role of Hamlet but the first night notices so unnerved him that before the curtain call on the second night he was taken ill and couldn't go on. The manager took the stage and asked the audience if they would suffer a production which omitted the character of Hamlet entirely. Sir Walter Scott, who was in the audience, said it was an improvement on the first night and many in the audience felt it was an improvement on the complete play.

★ ☆ ★

An actor playing John of Gaunt at the opening of *Richard II* was so drunk that he staggered about the stage on entrance without saying a word. The audience began to mutter uneasily as they rustled their programmes to see his name. He made his way unsteadily to the footlights, stared at the audience and said, 'If you think I'm pissed, just wait until you see the Duke of York.'

★ ☆ ★

Farce is what happens during the worst day of your life.

• Anon

★ ☆ ★

Trying to work out the personality of Shakespeare was like looking at a very dark picture under glass. At first you see nothing, then you begin to recognize features and then you recognize them as your own.

• Desmond McCarthy, Theatre Critic

★ ☆ ★

On the eve of the Millennium, we might ask if Shakespeare is much more than a conveniently empty box to put things in. His plays and poems have acquired an all-purpose quality which has gone way beyond that breadth of vision for which he was long revered, and which fans might once have dubbed the mark of his 'genius'.

Shakespeare has become a cypher, one of those iconic figures – alongside the likes of Jackie Kennedy, Marilyn Monroe, Albert

Einstein and Che Guevara – who can be filled with any consumer message you fancy.

Shakespeare is the hologram on your bank cash-card, you can purchase his image on-line on a tote-bag, he graces a durable apron, or as a comfy pillow for your settee. The National Portrait Gallery does a roaring trade in postcards of that famous painting with an earring, attributed to John Taylor, which might or might not be a likeness of our William.

• Lisa Jardine, *The Times*, 2.1.99

★ ☆ ★

Mr R C W Malim, of Blandford, Dorset, writes that he could just about, though with difficulty, accept that a 'provincial small tradesman, brought up speaking an accent almost unintelligible to London, possibly educated to the age of 14 maximum, saddled with a wife and three children before the age of 22 and in his father's failing business might conceivably throw it all up and emerge five years later as the completely rounded character and the greatest ornament to literature since writing was invented.

'What is totally unacceptable is that, having completed all this writing in a comparatively short space of time, he is not heard of again in London after 1604 and apparently – at the latest possible date of, say, 1611 – retires to Stratford-upon-Avon, takes no further interest in his own productions and goes back to buying bits of property and dunning small debtors, more especially as we are told in the 1623 folio introduction that death took him away before he had time to put his papers in order.'

• Frank Johnson, *Daily Telegraph*, 27.6.98

★ ☆ ★

'In a cold dark little room over against the back of the theatre, Sir Francis Bacon was talking eloquently. Opposite him a melancholy figure sat tracing its signature on a pad. Shakesper; Shakspere; Shekspar; he always practised tracing his signature when he was bored,' begins *No Bed For Bacon* by Caryl Brahms and S J Simon. Underlying the joke is the odd fact that all six of Shakespeare's surviving signatures are spelt differently: Willm Shakp, William Shakespe, Wm Shakesper, William Shakspere, William Shaksper.

Note that not one of the autographs spells Shakespeare's name the way we do. The official explanation for this embarrassing fact – which would surely cause havoc in the classroom if more widely known: 'Well at least I can spell better than Shakespeare, Miss' – is that Elizabethan surnames were not regarded as fixed.

Brahms and Simon settle for a more straightforward explanation, which is that Shakespeare was useless at spelling.

• John Lanchester, *Daily Telegraph*, 6.2.99, reviewing *No Bed for Bacon* by Caryl Brahams and S J Simon

★ ☆ ★

I'm on a crusade to try to persuade people that theatre can be fun, but every time I start doing that, some hairy bugger from the lift comes in and tells them it's intrusive, and drives them all out again. If I want to be instructed, I'll go to night school.'

• Alan Ayckbourn, interviewed by Rhoda Koenig, *Independent on Sunday*, 10.10.99

★ ☆ ★

What's a good show, asks a friend over from Los Angeles. Easy: *Closer* is great, but you may find the sex and language a bit visceral. No sweat, he says. The last show we saw in LA had a notice on the door: 'This play contains a little nudity and some smoking.' The curtain goes up, and a guy is sitting there butt naked – and then he lights up. You could hear gasps all over the theatre. At the interval, they posted another notice: 'Only herbal cigarettes used at this performance.'

• Peter Preston, *Guardian Weekend*, 18.7.98

★ ☆ ★

It is as *The Mousetrap*'s director that Peter Cotes created theatrical history. It wasn't that he was remembered strictly for his direction of the play, for the way he orchestrated its original production; not even his flatterers would argue that, though nearly all the first-night notices of 1952 paid tribute to the subtlety and atmosphere, timing and tension of his staging. The tribute paid to him as director ever since the play opened in Newcastle upon Tyne had nothing to do with the art of the theatre. It was his royalties. They constituted a 1.5 per cent share of the takings (which have amounted over the years to well over £25m). This kept him in the public eye.

• Obituary of Peter Cotes by Adam Benedick, *Independent*, 12.11.98

★ ☆ ★

The British have never cared for Jean Racine. He is the victim of Francophobia and Bardolatry. Even in his lifetime (1639-99), when French culture dominated the Continent even more than French arms, Racine was seen as a kind of literary Louis XIV: all rhetorical pomp and static tableaux. The caricature stuck. From Dryden to Garrick and Dr Johnson, the British proclaimed Shakespeare's pre-eminence over the French as if they were fighting for the Duke of Marlborough. Far more than Blenheim, their victory still resonates. When Goethe revived the German theatre, it was Shakespeare he followed, French neoclassicism he rejected. And while Hollywood has made dozens of Shakespeare movies, it has barely heard of Racine.

This three hundred years war of the theatre can even be quantified. Shakespeare uses some 21,000 words in his works;

Racine's vocabulary in his plays is said to be only 600. His miraculous economy of means is inimitable in English, just as Shakespeare's creative chaos is unthinkable in French. Where Shakespeare lives by taking liberties, Racine liberates by imposing rules. Unlike Shakespeare, who 'knew little Latin and less Greek', Racine was steeped in classical culture. When strict observance of the dramatic unities went out with the rise of Romanticism, Racine was left looking like an Aristotelian control freak.

As a result, London – the dramatic capital of the world – has hardly ever seen the works of one of the greatest dramatists of all time actually performed.

• Daniel Johnson, *The Times*, 12.11.98

★ ☆ ★

When *An Englishman Abroad* was shown in America the reaction was enthusiastic. Coral Browne attended a Hollywood party at which an indifferent writer came up to congratulate her. 'I loved your performance,' he cooed, 'and I thought Alan was superb...and John's direction was just exquisite...the only thing that worried me just a little, just a little, was the quality of the writing.'

'The quality of the writing?' she exploded. '*You* couldn't write "fuck" in the dust on a Venetian blind!'

• *Spectator*, 8.6.91

★ ☆ ★

The curtain rose on a simple setting dominated by a massive phallus. Coral Browne's comment cut through the shocked silence, 'NO ONE WE KNOW!'

• *Ibid*

★ ☆ ★

Many of the stories about Lew Grade are apocryphal. A true one he told against himself concerned the time he was watching a comedy act in the second half at the Metropolitan Theatre in the Edgware Road.

He thought it was top-of-the-bill material and rushed backstage. 'I'm Lew Grade. Your act was amazing. How much are they paying you?'

'£25 a week, Mr Grade.'

'Ridiculous. Absurd. Outrageous. I could get you £200. Who's your agent?'

'You are, Mr Grade.'

• *Sunday Times*, 20.12.98

* ☆ *

Mishcon de Reya, the City solicitors, held a fundraising evening this week for the refurbishment of the Royal Court Theatre. (Weird, the notion of the Establishment rallying to save that crucible of left-wing activism on Sloane Square; only this week we learnt of the Jerwood Foundation's £3 million donation.)

Actor Simon Russell Beale told a draughty Middle Temple hall that the Royal Court might be strapped for cash, but things were worse in the past. He read out a letter from George Bernard Shaw to the theatre's manager complaining of the cold.

Shaw said his wife was moved to tears, and as a result her eyelids froze shut. His mother passed out and could not be revived. In the stalls there was unrest over the lack of hooks for coats and hats, with one man saying if there had been a hook, he could at least have hanged himself to escape.

• City Diary, *The Times*, 5.12.98

* ☆ *

An incident in the career of the great actor-manager Donald Wolfit (1902-68) could provide some composer of today with a happy ending for *Macbeth*. Wolfit had sacked from his company the actor playing Seton who has scarcely more than the line: 'The Queen, my lord, is dead.'

When Wolfit, as Macbeth, asked the question in that evening's performance, the aggrieved actor replied: 'The Queen, my lord, is very much better.'

• Frank Johnson, *Daily Telegraph*, 16.1.99

★ ☆ ★

The Importance of Being Earnest is regarded as an artistically safe play: no sex, no swearing, no violence, no politics. The literary importance of *The Importance*, however, rests on anything but safeness. Oscar Wilde's text was virtually experimental in being perhaps the only comedy in history in which nearly every line, even of exposition or explanation, is a joke or a cue for a joke.

Prominent is the kind of epigram with which Wilde's writing is most associated, particularly in what might be called four-part disharmony, such as: 'All women become like their mothers. That is their tragedy. No man does. That is his.' This trick also frequently takes the form of inverted common wisdom, as when Gwendolen laments: 'Few parents nowadays pay any regard to what their children say to them. The old-fashioned respect for the young is fast dying out. Whatever influence I ever had over mamma, I lost at the age of three.'

The other Wildean trademark is metaphorical over-reaction, as when the news that John Worthing was found abandoned in a handbag at Victoria Station leads Lady Bracknell to object: 'You can hardly imagine that I and Lord Bracknell would dream of allowing our only daughter – a girl brought up with the utmost care – to marry into a cloakroom and form an alliance with a parcel.'

These joke structures are the foundation of 20th-century theatrical comedy in English. The line of descent from Wilde through Coward and Orton to Stoppard and Bennett is a clear one: each reworks the templates of Wilde's epigrams and exaggeration arias.

Tom Stoppard openly acknowledges the genealogy in *Travesties*, which is a parody of *the Importance of Being Earnest*, but a quieter debt is just as apparent in *Arcadia* when the overbearing Lady Croom comments of her precocious daughter: 'Thirteen years and ten months. She is not due to be pert for six months at the earliest, or to have notions of taste for much longer.'

• Mark Lawson, *Independent*, 14.2.95

★ ☆ ★

My Life With Noël Coward offers the occasional glint of buried treasure: the discovery that Coward wrote *Hay Fever* in three days and *Private Lives* in four; the fact that Mad Dogs and Englishmen was inspired when Coward was in Vietnam and the only whites out in the midday sun were French.

It is also awesome to learn that he turned down five of the most resonant parts of his time: Harry Lime in *The Third Man*, Professor Higgins in *My Fair Lady*, Colonel Nicholson in *The Bridge on the River Kwai*, the King in *The King and I*, and even Humbert Humbert in *Lolita*. 'Had he accepted these,' says Graham Payne, 'his later years might have been made much easier.'

• Graham Lord, reviewing *My Life With Noël Coward* by Graham Payne, *Daily Telegraph*, 12.12.94

★ ☆ ★

In October 1961, Keith Baxter had lunch with Margaret Leighton and Noël Coward in a German restaurant on West 44th Street. While Baxter was looking at the menu, Coward lowered his voice and observed conspiratorially: 'The food's good but the place is entirely staffed with Nazis. I whistle Rule Britannia and under-tip.'

• Paul Bailey, *Daily Telegraph*, 5.12.98

31 Too Important For Generals

war and the military

Old battles never die. They simply fade away into the names of railway stations. As our Paris correspondent reports, a French politician has written to Tony Blair demanding that he rename Waterloo Station. He declares that it is a standing insult to the French when they arrive in London by the Channel Tunnel, that they have to detrain at a station that commemorates the greatest British defeat of the French since Agincourt. If the British will not change Waterloo to a more *communautaire* name, Florent Longuepée threatens to rename the Gare du Nord 'Fontenoy'.

Now every French schoolchild knows that Fontenoy in 1745 was the last military victory of the French over the British. Of course, in the complex campaigns of the War of the Austrian Succession, this was a famous French victory.

But Fontenoy was fought in Flanders. And as usual, the British put a vexatious spin on their defeat. Cumberland excused his defeat by saying of the Wild Geese, the Irish mercenaries who had fought with the French: 'God's curse on the laws that made these men our enemies.' While the British infantry paused to dress ranks, Lord Charles Hay of the Grenadier Guards dashed forward and drank a toast to the French. Then, according to Voltaire, he shouted in Franglais: 'Gentleman of the French Guard, you have first shot!' And so they decimated the British front line.

So although Fontenoy was indeed a famous British defeat, the British have turned it into an heroic myth. This is not a battle that is on every English schoolchild's lips. Many will think it the misspelt name of a ballet dancer.

• Leader, *The Times*, 6.11.98

★ ☆ ★

Eighty-five years ago, my great-grandfather, the fifth Earl of Longford, died at Gallipoli. His last words to his second-in-command, who was crouching down to avoid the shells flying overhead, were: 'Please don't duck, Fred. It won't help you and it's no good for the men's morale.'

Soon after, Thomas Longford, advancing at the head of his Yeomanry Brigade troops with a map in one hand and a walking-stick in the other, fell in a hail of rifle fire. 'Fred' – Fred Cripps, brother of Sir Stafford, the future Chancellor of the Exchequer – survived for another 60 years. He was one of the lucky few: 21 of the 28 officers and all Longford's staff were killed. So heavy was the fire that bullet met bullet in mid-air – several of the squashed crosses of lead that were formed by these collisions are now in the Gallipoli museum.

• Harry Mount, *Spectator*, 22.4.00

★ ☆ ★

George III retorted to the man who told him that Wolfe of Quebec was thought to be insane: 'Then I wish he'd bite some of my other generals!'

• Andrew Roberts, *Sunday Telegraph*, 7.5.00

★ ☆ ★

During the retreat of the German Army in France in World War II, the following document written by the Education Officer of the 1st Parachute Division came into the hands of Monty's 8th Army Intelligence: 'Officers must counteract by all possible means and with conviction, the assertions made by the enemy, as well *as even some of our own people,* that the Fuhrer goes mad with rage and when he is in that state tears down curtains, bites the carpet in his rage and rolls in convulsions on the floor. There are witnesses who know that Hitler is well above such lack of control, though many a man in the street, if he were exposed to the disappointments and grief which the Fuhrer has to bear, would have gone under long ago.'

The date is significant: 20 September 1944. After the July 20th plot and when the German Army was in full retreat and we were bombarding the retreating armies with black defeatist propaganda. No German officer would have written such a memo and expect to be alive for very long. The real stamp of our Black Propaganda Department is in evidence.

• Canadian Army Intelligence Report

★ ☆ ★

The final decision of war is not always absolute. The conquered nation often sees it only as a passing evil to be repaired in the future by political combinations.

• Clausewitz

★ ☆ ★

'But what good came of it at last?'
Quoth little Peterkin.
'Why, that I cannot tell,' said he,
'But 'twas a famous victory.'

• Robert Southey, from The Battle of Blenheim (1800)

32 To Women, Equality Is Being Like A Man

women

You're stupid. I like that in a woman.

• Caption to cartoon in the *New Yorker* by Whitney Darrow Jr

★ ☆ ★

If women didn't exist, all the money in the world would have no meaning.

• Aristotle Onassis, quoted by Luke Johnson, *Sunday Telegraph*, 9.1.00

★ ☆ ★

The tale that interested me this week has to do with a lady called Ananova. You have probably never heard of her. That is because she does not exist. She is the creation of computer programmers in Silicon Valley and she is a newsreader, designed to deliver information on the internet 24 hours a day, seven days a week. She is the perfect news presenter: beautiful, relaxed, intelligent and infallible. This truly sensational development was entirely ignored by my colleagues in television newsrooms.

I am not surprised. Ananova never fluffs her lines and never demands the sort of stratospheric salary paid to my more fortunate colleagues across the Atlantic. She never throws a tantrum, never demands more sympathetic lighting in the studio or a bigger dress allowance and she never says embarrassing things about her bosses to newspaper interviewers. Yet not only is she the answer to a harassed bureaucrat's prayers, she is completely in keeping with the times.

You say that all she will do is regurgitate the words fed her by others, that she will never stray off message and display a rebellious streak. I say in that case she is no different from half the politicians who presently occupy our screens. You say she will inevitably mouth formulaic platitudes. I ask if you have ever heard a modern businessman after he has swallowed the contents of his favourite guru's latest theories. You say that surely we like the sound of the human voice. I suggest you count the number of times in a typical day when you are informed or instructed by the metallic, disembodied voice telling you which buttons to press on your telephone or what floor your lift has arrived at or why there is not the smallest chance of you being connected with the person you had hoped to deal with.

• John Humphries, *Guardian*, 23.1.00

★ ☆ ★

An investigation into the contents of women's handbags reveals that some contain as many as 44 items. That does not surprise me. I divide women into two types. The first has a lot of handbags, empties them often, selects the one she plans to use, cleans the insides, and inserts the contents on strict criteria of utility and logic, usually no more than half a dozen, which nowadays would include a palmtop or, in America, a gun as well. This kind of woman is formidable, reliable, handy; not necessarily warm, though. The other type has one, much bigger bag, which she lugs around with her on all occasions, except evening parties when she clutches a velvet wisp and has a bereaved look. Such bags – the French term *sac* is better – contain various archaeological layers, ending in a Pleistocene of grunge: dogeared bus tickets, half-eaten chocs, tiny, worthless foreign coins, buttons, aspirins, chewing gum, grimy bits of lipstick, a pencil stub (won't write), angrily crumpled bills, sometimes a prize item like a tearstained letter, much read and folded, from a lover long long ago – the whole bound together by a glue of crumbs, powder, hair and sticky sweet-papers. I have known such bags contain a quarter-bottle of gin (empty), a diamond-studded dog-collar, a child's odd shoe, a pair of pliers, a 20-year-old election manifesto and a hairless teddy bear. These women will keep you waiting but will hug you tight.

Handbags go back a long way and have sometimes contained grisly items, such as the head of Holofernes, still dripping. I would like to have poked around in Cleopatra's to see what it harboured: charms, charms, charms, I daresay, and a handy asp if they failed to work. Queen Elizabeth had a girdle-bag, or pouch, containing miniature editions of Seneca, verses by Petrarch, writing materials, sweets and herbal remedies, which she gave to her privy counsellors to save them from the horrors of Tudor medicine. What did Mary Queen of Scots have in hers? She was an archaeological-layers-of-grunge woman, and among the deposits would have been found homemade poisons, an archive of treasonable letters, and perhaps even a tiny live dog, like the one that crept out from under her petticoats when her head was chopped off.

Literary ladies do not necessarily conform to bluestocking archetypes. In my experience their bags contain an astonishing amount of aids to vanity, bits of underwear or even outerwear discarded in moments of panic, false eyelashes, hopelessly jammed bottles of nail varnish, broken bits of jewellery, rusty nail-files, as well as a complete pharmacopoeia. Not, as you might expect, pocket editions of Shakespeare, Roget's *Thesaurus*, Greek dictionaries etc. Jane Austen's handbag, I imagine, would be worth a book in itself: very large but not at all grungy, and fitted out according to utilitarian principles (she was a contemporary of Jeremy Bentham) with everything that might be needed by a lady with a passionate interest in clothes forced by circumstances to make her own. Thus, she would have India tape, scraps of jute webbing, piping cord, press-studs, needles galore (and needle-threaders in later life), ric-rac, seam-binding, markers and mending wool, thread snips, thimbles, twist-pins, curlifil, bodkins and bump interlining, a darning mushroom, slivers of Hessian and Russian braid, Guterman threads and Offray ribbons, slipping-thread, silesia and small squares of felt. Plenty of bobbins, too, dressmaker's pins, Bolton twill, beeswax, scrim and gimp-braids, with maybe Cassandra's latest letter crowning the whole.

• Paul Johnson, *Spectator*, 27.11.99

★ ☆ ★

There's nothing like the atmosphere in Karen Millen or Whistles or Jigsaw or – when our boat sporadically comes in – Nicole Farhi. You sit there, surrounded by women, the only man, utterly accepted and yet also wonderfully different.

It's like you've been given a day-pass into the harem. Except they can't complain, no one runs screaming for the eunuchs – you're invisible, you're immaterial, you're the licensed observer. And you have the time to observe, the freedom to soak up that exotically hyper-female atmosphere.

And what you see is womankind observing itself, concentrating on itself, readying itself for the cut and thrust of the sexual piste. What could be, for a man, more watchable?

• Jonathan Myerson, on clothes-shopping with his wife. *Independent*, 6.10.98

★ ☆ ★

Barbarella, Jean-Claude Forest's girl of tomorrow was truly liberated, needing no cumbersome spacesuit to survive in the vastness of space. A pair of droopy pantomime boots and an even droopier bikini was all she needed to protect herself from every spacial hazard from meteorites to monstrosities. The strip gained huge popularity and in 1964 the first set of strips was reprinted as a book by the French publishers Frank Losfeld. Two years later Grove Press translated an edition for America. Meanwhile the French authorities anxious that their country would not become the world's publishing centre for pornography once again banned it. The US edition escaped censure and *Newsweek* reviewed Forest's strip thus:

'Cruising among the planets like a female James Bond, Barbarella vanquishes evil and rewards, in her own particular way, all the handsome men she meets in outer space. And whether she is tussling with Strikno the sadistic hunter, or turning her ray-gun on weird gelatinous monsters, she just cannot seem to avoid losing part or all of her skin-tight spacesuit.'

• Obituary of cartoonist Jean-Claude Forest, by Denis Gifford, *Independent*, 1.1.99

★ ☆ ★

Japan's first robot waitress went to work in a restaurant near Tokyo last Tuesday. Named Meimei, or little sister, she is adept at bringing menus and glasses of water, but has not sufficiently mastered voice recognition to take orders. Moving on six wheels, wearing a pink kimono and speaking in a high-pitched voice, she is programmed to issue a caution if customers attempt to touch her moving parts. In this event, she assumes a worried expression and summons assistance.

• Stop the Week, *The Sunday Times*, 30.4.00

★ ☆ ★

A woman who is ostentationally vain about her flower-like beauty should be given a hot water bottle for Christmas or a small, biscuit-coloured Shetland shawl to wear in bed or a tin of

patent food which announces clearly on the label that it has been specifically treated to make it more easily digestible.
• Stephen Potter

★ ☆ ★

Never lie down with a woman who's got more problems than you.
• Algren's Precepts

Vicky

33 Marilyn And Lettuce

work, business and advertising

Her harasser never laid a finger on her. Neither did he say anything suggestive. Indeed he never said anything to her at all: the man and the woman he allegedly harassed had never even met.

But she had a case nevertheless, or so the judge decided. The man in question had had sex with *other* women in the office and this had led to their promotion. The victim claimed that because she had *not* been invited to have sex with the guy she had missed out on promotion.

This, thank goodness, is not the real world, but the kooky, whimsical world of *Ally McBeal*. Last week's episode boldly went where no prime-time US sitcom has gone before and dared to make fun of the lucrative and ludicrous realm of sexual harassment litigation.

The present position in the US – which you might have thought beyond ridicule – is that if you say anything which could be construed as salacious or which could conceivably create a hostile working environment, you can be taken to court and to the cleaners.

And so too can your employer, even if it did not have the foggiest idea of what was going on. This new slant on the law has put the wind up some companies so badly that they are sending all new recruits off on a *two-week* training course to wash all the potentially offensive behaviour out of them, before they are deemed safe to join the workforce.

Set against all that, I wonder how funny US reviewers found *Ally McBeal.* My worry is that for every person who watched it, squirmed and laughed, there will be another for whom it will have provided ideas about new ways of milking the system.

• Lucy Kellaway, *Financial Times*, 5.10.98

* ☆ *

There is no more persuasive industry in America than PR. I first contacted it when I interviewed Marilyn Monroe in Phoenix, Arizona in April, 1955.

It was a hot day in Phoenix. The publicity man for Twentieth Century Fox, Roy Craft, stripped to the waist, bent confidentially over the telephone he was cuddling in both hands. He nodded to me to sit down.

'We'd be plumb delighted to have Marilyn photographed with the Governor and the little girl,' he was saying. 'If he could come round before the parade – either on or off his horse – we could take them in front of the cameras. I know Marilyn would just love to have her picture taken with that sick child – so long as it doesn't interfere with the shooting – understand. And, honey, we're only too happy to do anything for the Governor of Arizona.' Roy Craft hung up, shook my hand and introduced me to three cowboys, two photographers, an assistant Press Agent, and a man in a blue suit. The small hotel room was rather crowded.

I had just flown into Phoenix where the first day's shooting of her new picture, *Bus Stop,* was to take place against a background of a mammoth parade and a 'world championship' rodeo organized by the city's Chamber of Commerce. It would be the first time she had appeared in front of the cameras since her walkout from Twentieth Century Fox almost a year and a half ago. The atmosphere was anxious.

'That was the Governor's secretary,' said Craft, the press agent, letting us all in on the telephone conversation. 'There's one of Marilyn's fans – a little girl – who has just had a serious operation. She is still in a state of deep depression and her doctor thinks that meeting Marilyn might snap her out of it. The girl's father is a friend of the Governor of Arizona and the Governor's office wants to know if we can take a picture of the Governor and the girl with Marilyn. He's leading the parade on a horse tomorrow so I'm trying to arrange it before we start moving. The little girl is driving up specially from Louisiana just for this. Amazing the effect Marilyn has on people! Ought to be good for the picture, too.'

The telephone rang again. It was a reporter on a local newspaper. The three cowboys stood up, mumbled some thanks for the drinks and slouched out. 'Not real cowboys,' said the assistant press agent when they'd gone. 'Just Chamber of Commerce boys dressed up to give the town some colour.'

'Yes, we've spoken to Marilyn about that matter,' said Craft on the telephone, 'and she assured us that the police escort seemed to be going at a normal, safe speed. She doesn't think they could have been travelling at fifty-five miles an hour and she didn't see them go through any red lights. And she hopes no one gets into any trouble over it.'

The press agent hung up with a wry smile and shrugged his shoulders. 'That girl doesn't need anybody to get her publicity. It just happens to her,' he said.

'Now I don't know much about what's been going on around here,' said the tall man in the blue suit, standing up and looming over Craft's desk. He had been silently nursing a Bourbon-and-soda in a corner, 'but do you think there's any chance of getting Marilyn's cooperation for my proposition?'

'Well, I'm sorry, Mr Anderson,' began the press agent.

'*Morrison*,' said the man in the blue suit.

'Mr Morrison,' said the press agent, 'but as you see we've been in a kind of hassle around here today and it's slipped my mind. Now could you brief me on it again?'

'It's an idea for publicising lettuce,' said Morrison. 'I represent the lettuce growers of Arizona and that's pretty big business. You ought to meet some of these lettuce kings. Why, Texas oil millionaires and film magnates have got nothing on them. Now I admit I don't know much about film stars and how you can tie lettuce up with them, but I thought it would be a good stunt if we could have Marilyn Monroe sponsor a crate of lettuce to be sent to Grace Kelly on her coming wedding day. All Marilyn would have to do is have her photograph taken with the crate of lettuce and two important lettuce growers. We'd look after sending the lettuce and everything else. I frankly don't know what Grace Kelly would do with the lettuce. Probably dump it into the Mediterranean. But we just want the public to realize the size and importance of the lettuce business.'

The press agent looked doubtful.

'Well, it may be alright for the lettuce growers and Grace Kelly, but what good will it do Marilyn?' he said. 'You see we can't have the public thinking Marilyn sent Grace a crate of lettuce for a wedding present. That's a pretty small gift for a girl in her position.'

'Oh, we can fix that all right,' replied Mr Morrison, eagerly. 'We can fly a whole airplane like a DC9 full of lettuce to Monaco, if you like. No one's worrying about the cost.'

The press agent still looked doubtful. When I left the room some fifteen minutes later they were still discussing it. The lettuce man seemed to be losing.

• Milton Shulman

★ ☆ ★

British manufacturers are constantly being criticized for their lack of drive and initiative in the export market. Get out and investigate your market, Government officials keep urging them, and find out what the locals actually want. Don't try and sell balalaikas to the Russians. The Vladivar vodka company instituted an Incredible Export Award for the company selling the most unlikely products to the most unlikely countries. The competition was reported in the *Export Times* and the winner was the Premier Drum Company of Leicester which successfully exports maracas to Caracas and bongos to the Congo.

The present contenders include a Halifax company which sells prayer mats to Mecca, a Birmingham firm that makes electrical ignitions for the modern hubble-bubble pipe most often smoked in Turkey, and a Manchester maker of yoga mats sold through a yoga institute in Poona.

A contender in Surrey exports sun-lamps to Australia and a firm in Oldham sells Swiss rolls in Switzerland. A Merseyside firm does a thriving business selling chow mein in Hong Kong while a Croydon company makes artificial sponges for customers in Tahiti and the Seychelles.

With initiative like that you can't write Britain off just yet. I wouldn't be surprised to discover there are energetic British firms peddling beefburgers in the Argentine, suntan lotion in Nigeria and peanuts for cocktail parties at the White House.

• *The Times* June 1977

★ ☆ ★

When Burger King, the second biggest hamburger chain in America opened its first branch in London in 1977, it set off an advertising war between rival hamburger companies in England. Wimpeys in their advertisements boasted that they sold seventy million hamburgers last year which was converted into 200,000,000 pieces of beef in buns. McDonald's retaliated with their claim that if someone started in 1977 to eat every hamburger that McDonald's ever made, assuming he took five minutes to chew each bun, he would still be munching them 228,000 years from now. They also informed us that the amount of beef used by McDonald's for their production of 24 billion hamburgers would amount to a herd of cattle standing shoulder to shoulder in an area twice the size of Greater London. An incidental fact revealed by their advertising duel was that the word hamburger had nothing to do with ham but was named after the town of Hamburg in Pennsylvania.

• Jane Hanning, *Daily Mail,* Oct 1977

★ ☆ ★

Advertising has annihilated the power of the most powerful adjectives – wonderful, magnificent, unbeatable.

★ ☆ ★

Two leading recipes for success are building a better mousetrap and finding a bigger loophole.

• Anon

★ ☆ ★

The gadget makes us all the same.

★ ☆ ★

It's when they go wrong that machines remind us how powerful they are.

★ ☆ ★

Work expands so as to fill the time available for its completion.

• Parkinson's Law

★ ☆ ★

If anything can go wrong, it will.

• Murphy's Law

★ ☆ ★

No experiment is ever a complete failure. It can always be used as a bad example.

• Carter's Consolation

★ ☆ ★

A hot-air balloonist realizes he is lost. He spots a man down below, reduces height and shouts: 'Excuse me, can you tell me where I am?'

The man below says: 'Yes, you're in a basket below a hot-air balloon, hovering 30 feet above this field.'

'You must work in information technology,' says the balloonist.

'I do,' replies the man. 'How did you know?'

'Well,' says the balloonist, 'everything you have told me is technically correct, but it's no use to anyone.'

The man below says, 'You must be a corporate manager.'

'I am,' replies the balloonist, 'but how did you know?'

'Well,' says the man, 'you don't know where you are, or where you're going, but you expect me to help. You're in the same position you were before we met, but now it's my fault.'

• Observer, *Financial Times*, 1.9.98

Index Of Sources

Index Of Sources

Internet:	**www.houseofstratus.com** including author interviews, reviews, features.
Email:	**sales@houseofstratus.com** **info@houseofstratus.com** (please quote author, title and credit card details.)
Tel:	**Order Line** **0800 169 1780 (UK)** **International** **+44 (0) 1845 527700 (UK)**
Fax:	**+44 (0) 1845 527711 (UK)** (please quote author, title and credit card details.)
Send to:	**House of Stratus Sales Dept.** **Thirsk Industrial Park** **York Road, Thirsk** **North Yorkshire, YO7 3BX** **UK**